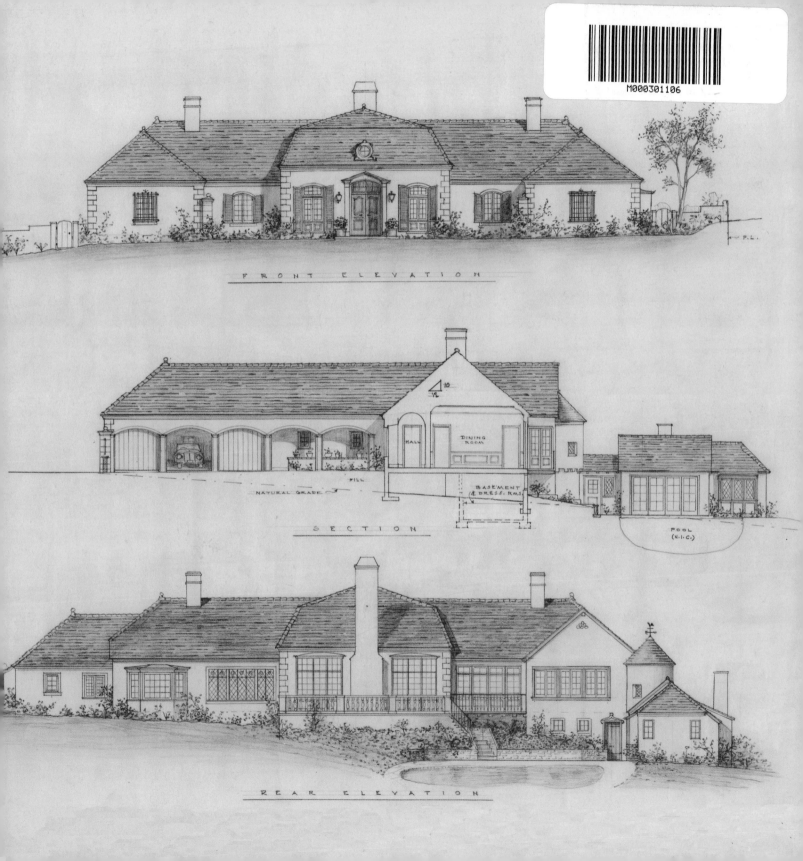

F R O N T   E L E V A T I O N

S E C T I O N

HALL

DINING
ROOM

FILL

NATURAL GRADE

BASEMENT
(& DRESS. RMS)

POOL
(N.I.C.)

R E A R   E L E V A T I O N

HOME
COLCORD

ANGEL CITY PRESS

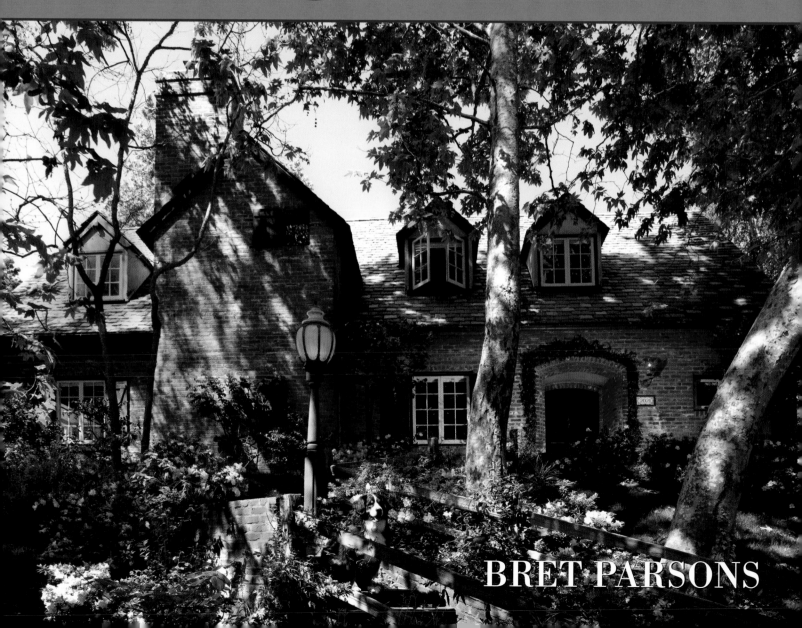

HOME
COLCORD

BRET PARSONS

Entrance courtyard at Trippet House, 1930, Pacific Palisades.

DEDICATED TO

Mary Ann Shemdin, who asked, "Why not a book just on Gerard Colcord?"

Ward Jewell, who asked, "Who's your favorite architect?"

Stephanie Stern, who confirmed what a valuable project this would be

Liza Kent, who safeguarded the archives

and

James & Sharon Parsons, who fostered the architectural predilections of a youngster

2006 image of Johnson House, 1936, Stone Canyon

CONTENTS

Chambers House, 1935,
Beverly Hills.
Pennsylvania Dutch-
style home has had
several owners, including
producer Tony Thomas.

PREFACE

No matter what taste or architectural style resonates with an individual, almost everyone responds emotionally to the work of architect Gerard Colcord. Whether he was designing a "Hansel and Gretel" cottage, a country farmhouse, or a stately English Tudor, the beauty of each home was conveyed not by mere ornamentation but by structural complexity and elemental design. Beauty was an undisputed necessity in every Colcord home. The rich textures of the Colcord style are uniquely identifiable: washed brick, honey-colored fieldstone, half-timbered beams, asymmetrical roof lines, hand-painted tiles and his signature walk-in fireplaces—all blending effortlessly and harmoniously.

Throughout the vast Southern California landscape are numerous examples of Gerard Colcord's work. His intimate cottage style became iconic during the 1930s, 1940s

The intimate den, decorated by second owner Jacquelyn M. Ross, features the famous "Colcord Beam" which is actually cement.

and 1950s. This was at a time when his contemporaries, H. Roy Kelly, Wallace Neff, and Gordon Kaufmann were designing massive Georgian, Mediterranean, and Spanish homes, and visionaries such as Richard Neutra, Rudolf Schindler and Frank Lloyd Wright were building bold, contemporary residences. But clients sought out Gerard Colcord when they wanted warmth, intimacy and romance.

His signature style is seductive; storybook adventure awaits in each authentic room. Colcord's focus was clear: to create a counterpoint to the mega-mansions of his day. It has been said that an extraordinary house, like a great novel or a priceless painting, can embrace the spirit and imagination of an entire era. That is exactly what Colcord achieved. He touched our deepest sensibilities with his magical and romantic vocabulary.

Ron de Salvo
Beverly Hills

PREFACE

9

PROLOGUE

Sisken House, 1946,
Beverly Hills.
This charming Colonial
Revival farmhouse-style
home, once the residence of
Hollywood manager Bernie
Brillstein, is home to a
collector with impeccable taste
in both furnishings and pets.

A passion for houses, their interiors, and surroundings must have genetic roots.

My Indiana-born grandmother Carmen Stevens and her husband Bill Radtke, a contractor, built their northern California home in 1952. She wanted a classic brick Federal; he wanted a serviceable box, a popular style after World War II. They fought a lot. Nevertheless, a compromise was reached with a Cliff May-inspired ranch house featuring two walk-in Colonial-style fireplaces, pegged-and-grooved random-width plank floors, and one of the bathrooms copied exactly from a design by Royal Barry Wills, the much admired Boston architect who was a master of Cape Cod. It all worked.

Still, Bill hated those fireplaces, and said so, until the weight of sincere compliments from friends and visitors about their beauty shifted his attitude to: "Yes, Carmen and I think they are the highlights of the house."

Carmen was really an artist, although she didn't know it. When asked by a friend how she always made the most pleasing aesthetic choice—whether it was for an antique, a painting, or even a sofa, she replied, "I walked through the woods to school as a child." Exactly. All art derives from the colors, textures, rhythms and forms of nature and she accessed that knowledge intuitively.

Later, when my brother and I spent summer vacations with Carmen and Bill, I drew floor plans—files full of them. Carmen would occasionally look over my shoulder and encourage me. She once said, "Bill never made the rooms in this place big enough. You better add twenty feet to the living room on your plan." She thought big.

One hot August afternoon I noticed a copy of *House & Garden* magazine on the kitchen counter. The cover featured a bright, comfortable living room in a rambling farmhouse built along the Napa River in Rutherford, California. The house had stone floors, beam ceilings, wrap-around porches, and multi-paned windows set into dormers that punctuated the hundred-foot wide roofline. The owners were an immensely successful businessman, Al Wilsey (he invented "butter pats"—pre-sliced butter placed upon tiny waxed paper squares), and his fashionable wife, the noted author, activist and socialite Pat

Pat Montandon stands in the Michael Taylor-designed living room at River Meadow Farm, her 1975 Colcord-inspired country home in Rutherford, California.

Opposite: Vaughn House, 1969, Stone Canyon. Everage Design elegantly furnished the baronial living room for new owners Wendy & Tony Cassara in 1987, only after the Vaughns had the entire home precisely replicated in Coeur d'Alene, Idaho. Actors Reese Witherspoon and Ryan Phillippe would be subsequent owners.

Montandon. The San Francisco architecture firm of Porter & Steinwedell developed the thirty-acre estate with home interiors created by designer Michael Taylor. An undulating lawn cascaded down to the river (past the carp pond, tennis courts, stables, and swimming pool) and was the setting of a house blessing party at which Benny Goodman entertained. Hold this picture, and fast-forward twenty-six years to October 2003.

During a visit with Pasadena Realtor Mary Ann Shemdin, our conversation largely concerned regional architecture and architects. We remembered and admired the work of Paul Williams, George Washington Smith, James Dolena, Wallace Neff and others. She suddenly remarked: "I love Gerard Colcord." I casually mentioned that one day I would like to write a book about favorite Los Angeles architects, plural. Shemdin asked, very matter-of-factly: "Why not a book *just* on Gerard Colcord?" I was intrigued, but my attention drifted back to my career as a mortgage broker and to renovating a Spanish duplex I owned at the time.

In January 2006, through a mutual friend, I met Pat Montandon (remember the "undulating lawn cascading past the carp pond . . . ?"). Conversation focused upon the magnificent homes that played starring roles during her married life. When she inquired about my book, I said it featured a Beverly Hills-based architect named Gerard Colcord who did extraordinary residential work during his sixty-year career.

She examined pictures of the homes I anticipated including and said with amazement, "In the early 1970s, I often visited Los Angeles in conjunction with a television show I hosted. During one trip I had an afternoon free, so, I rented a car and drove up and down the streets around the Beverly Hills Hotel taking pictures of homes I felt drawn to—you know—to get ideas for the country house Al and I were planning to build. Bret, your images are the houses I took pictures of. They became the models for River Meadow Farm." Another mysterious moment of synchronicity. When they arrive, it's best to pay attention because doors have begun to open.

During the summer of 2006, I had lunch with Westwood architect Ward Jewell, who asked me to name my favorite architect. I said, "Besides you, Ward, it's Gerard Colcord." He encouraged me to visit Colcord-owning clients of his. One of those clients led me to Liza Kent, the architectural designer who ran Mr. Colcord's business from 1970 until he died in 1984. I spent an energetic afternoon with Liza, much like a kid in a candy store as she showed me architectural documents she had stored for over twenty years. I finally had to leave, but during the drive home, I simultaneously conceptualized, wrote, designed

Daisy-Rose warmly greeted the author during many visits.

and published a book on Colcord. However, when I pulled into the garage and turned off the ignition, I sat there realizing my only true accomplishment over the past two hours of drive time was mentally creating a book. Then I thought, "Now what?"

The "Now what?" turned into over three hundred interviews with an extraordinary cast of Southern California characters, many of whom are current Colcord homeowners. They include developers, executives, a couple of moguls, religious leaders, a veterinarian, celebrities, realtors, architects, interior designers, writers, lawyers (lots of lawyers), a few movie stars, retirees, homemakers, an orchestra conductor, and educators. They were all engaging, friendly and eager to help (with only one vivid exception, which proves the rule). Former Colcord owners waxed poetic about owning the "most favorite home" they ever lived in. Remember that poignant moment in *E.T.* when the little extra-terrestrial points his finger and longingly said, "Hooommmeee"? For many, Colcord homes inspire the same longing and devotion.

Colcord estates are full of charm and inherent personality, located in sought-after neighborhoods. The style of these residences implies an idyllic life: a joyful affluent family, tasteful interiors, gourmet aromas from the kitchen, manicured gardens, perfectly behaved children, friendly obedient pets, and neighbors warmly greeted as they drop in unexpectedly.

And, actually, this is true to a very large degree: Colcord did create storybook homes built in desirable Southern California communities. Families that live in them are successful and fun. Interiors range from exceedingly "old money comfortable" to camera-ready perfect. And, oftentimes, friends, family and staff members breezily waltzed in and out. The kids were friendly, and nearly every Colcord has a plethora of pets with which I was on a first-name basis.

A Colcord home exemplifies the conclusion of one architectural critic when he spoke about a beautiful home, "The space is so right you have to become a better person living in it."

Welcome to *Colcord Home*.

BRET PARSONS
Los Angeles, California
2008

Opposite: Colcord was adroit at siting homes in their optimum location. The 1930s San Fernando Valley looms below this sprawling one-story Spanish hacienda, another style Colcord masterfully interpreted.

INTRODUCTION

"Men like Gerard Colcord aren't made anymore," enthused Gladys Boynton, whose husband Wayne, a Southern California real-estate developer, built many Colcord homes. "Gerry, the name his friends called him, was a fabulous, delightful, thoughtful man with a marvelous intellect, who appreciated a good time, and dressed beautifully, often in tweed jackets. We absolutely adored him. Not a Hollywood type at all, he was refined, much like an English country gentleman."

Once known only to a small, yet informed group of affluent Angelenos, Colcord designed nearly three hundred homes and remodeled one hundred more. Most of them are located in a particularly rich architectural environment in Southern California from San Marino to the east, Malibu to the west, Chatsworth to the north, and Palos Verdes Estates to the south.

Rather than courting publicity and fame, Colcord focused on creating an extraordinary array of highly detailed, superbly crafted residences. His designs ranged from classic Tudors and Colonial Revivals to Country French, Hollywood Regency, Spanish Hacienda, Monterey Colonial, and even contemporary. After World War II, charming "Country Colonials" would emerge as his signature genre, which continue to inspire fortunate homeowners and their guests to this day. For exactly six decades, he "quietly plied his trade in the shadow of the burgeoning Modern movement" says noted Los Angeles architect Marc Appleton. "Like many other local architects who chose to work in traditional or regional styles, Colcord's extraordinary architectural achievement was largely unheralded by his peers. Colcord's houses were modest yet romantic and eminently livable exercises in traditional styles. His homes are appealing not just for their architectural statement but for the family life they nurture."

Seventy-year-old Gerard Colcord with Stephanie Sax at the groundbreaking for her house on April 18, 1972, in Studio City.

Trippet House,
Pacific Palisades,
1930, viewed
from the driveway.
Designing the
side elevations of
homes was just
as important to
Colcord as the front
and rear façades.

Colcord's classic
Colonial interior
details, shown
here, were often
reinterpreted, although
seldom successfully,
by Southern
California speculative
homebuilders.

Many architects say they consider Colcord a genius, and that it would be rare for anyone to practice at Colcord's level of detail and precision today. Not surprisingly, Colcord's homes were frequently copied by speculative home builders. Knock-offs abound, often passed off as "authentic Colcords" by unknowing or disinterested Realtors, and sell for millions of dollars. Realty firms selling "architectural properties" are now required to have original building permits on file to verify authenticity.

SOUTHERN CALIFORNIA RESIDENTIAL BUILDING HISTORY

Southern California offers an extraordinary choice of home styles. One may choose to live in a shingled beach house overlooking the Pacific Ocean, a ranch house in the San Fernando Valley, a chic steel-and-glass aerie poised over Hollywood, a cozy creek-side Craftsman bungalow in Pasadena, or a palatial Beverly Hills mansion once occupied by a famous—or infamous—celebrity. And these possibilities are all within a short drive of one another.

Ironically, Southern California as it is constituted today should technically not exist. Only imported water, via an elaborate aqueduct system credited to William Mulholland, enables life to flourish. Residents inhabit a irrigated desert which in turn provides extraordinary weather and fosters exemplary building conditions.

These elements, plus the economic powerhouse of the emerging movie and aerospace industries, led to the almost overnight development of the region at the turn of the twentieth century. Small, scattered ranchos disappeared as new residential developments showcased the latest in Mediterranean villas and Spanish cottages. Even houses that had no direct relation to the topography—Tudor castles, traditional Colonials and French chateaux—were erected, often by entertainment-industry folk. By the 1920s, Art Deco, eclectic historicism, Beaux Arts, and fantasy architecture sprouted all over Southern California appearing in the form of private homes, apartment complexes and department stores.

This artistic climate incubated architectural practitioners whose homes are still sought. Ranch houses by Cliff May, revivalist designs by Roland E. Coate, Garrett Van Pelt, Jr., and John Byers, and moderns by Richard Neutra, Lloyd Wright and Rudolph Schindler all lived in companionable harmony.

Commencing in 1924, Colcord quietly began an architectural practice in Beverly Hills and, by his death in 1984, he had created an unprecedented array of residential jewel boxes, not palaces. His designs spanned centuries and, while most were not historically accurate, the houses that emerged were a combination of the most picturesque qualities culled from architectural details around the world, skillfully blended and tailored for lifestyles of the day.

THE PERSONAL COLCORD

Gerard Rae Colcord was born November 1, 1900, in St. Louis, Missouri, to Walter Rae Colcord and Meta Eliza Garrells Colcord. Eight years later, his sister Eunice was born. The Colcord family enjoyed a privileged lifestyle. Walter was president of the Doris Motor Company of St. Louis, and one of the city's most prominent industrialists. Previously he had been the president of Colcord–Wright Machinery Company and a director of the Franklin Bank of St. Louis. Meta, of French ancestry, was an accomplished artist and would later paint many of the decorative tiles her son placed in kitchens, bathrooms, and on fireplace surrounds.

Colcord's artistic inclinations emerged when he was just a boy. One of his favorite activities was to sit on the stair landing of his banker grandfather's Tudor mansion in St. Louis and watch how the setting sun illuminated the stained glass and cast designs throughout the room.

Colcord, like other sons from affluent families in the early twentieth century, was sent to boarding school for his high school education. His parents chose the respected Culver Military Academy in Indiana. According to his yearbook, he was well-liked and excelled at archery. One might speculate that the dexterity he exhibited as an archer translated into his ability to quickly create lifelike drawings for which he was later lauded. Colcord graduated from Culver's "Black Horse Troop" in spring 1920.

Around this same time, patriarch Walter, age forty-seven, moved the family to Beverly Hills. Colcord returned to Los Angeles, moved into the new family home and,

Gerard R. Colcord
St. Louis, Mo.

LELAND-STANFORD—
SCIENTIFIC

17-18—Pvt. Co. R. Co. Football
18-19—Pvt. Co. B. Co. Swimming.
19-20—Pvt. Co. B. Co. Swimming.
Boxing, Varsity Rifle Team, YMCA.
Two Stripe Club

Water and love are dangerous. Gean has been in both them over his head, and no lifesavers or preservers can rescue him. His only regret is that the pool was out of commission so much of the time this year. However, he has been active along other lines and is one of the best shots on the rifle team. He has won a place in the esteem of all the men in Argonne and leaves, well remembered by everybody. He is a man who will be much missed in the regiment.

A graduate of Culver Military Academy in Indiana, Colcord counted among his classmates Horace M. Heidt, who would become a famed bandleader and land developer in the San Fernando Valley.

Left: A portrait book of buildings at Fontainebleau, where Colcord studied, was a treasured keepsake.
Right: Colcord's diploma from Fontainebleau was granted in October 1924. He returned to Beverly Hills to begin his practice at age twenty-four.

by the fall of 1920, enrolled at the University of Southern California. In 1923, Colcord continued his education at the prestigious École des Beaux-Arts in Paris.

The French college was founded in 1648 to develop studies in drawing, painting, sculpture, engraving, modeling and gem cutting. The architecture division was added in 1671. The school was brought under the control of the French government by Louis XIV, originally to guarantee a pool of artists available to decorate the palaces and paint members of royalty. It was made independent by Napoleon III in 1863. Entrance requirements were rigorous. Foreigners were discouraged from applying, and only admitted under strict quotas, which were never publicly defined. Colcord was part of a newly established, one-year apprentice program at the École des Beaux-Arts at Fontainebleau.

"[Fontainebleau] was built in 1528 onwards around the keep of a small medieval chateau. The work was carried out in several stages that lasted until the eighteenth century; hence the irregularity in plan and lack of unity in style," according to John Julius Norwich in *The World Atlas of Architecture*. Colcord's apprenticeship there would completely define his subsequent design perspective: creating homes by incorporating disparate elements from many centuries, all mixed into a unified and pleasing whole. Colcord graduated, and on October 14, 1924, sailed from Marseilles, France, on the ship *Patria*, to New York City. He traveled to Beverly Hills, moved back into the family home and commenced his practice at age twenty-four.

OVERVIEW OF CAREER

Early on, Colcord possessed the qualities necessary for an unusually successful career. First, he accommodated and pleased his clients by being scrupulously thorough. Before designing a house he closely examined and evaluated the building site. Next he studied the family who would inhabit the property and learned what they desired. Then he referred to his files of torn-out magazine pages from periodicals including *American Architect and Architecture*, *The Architect & Engineer*, *Architecture*, *Arts & Decoration*, *California Arts & Architecture*, and *The House Beautiful* for specific details. Only then did he produce a floor plan with an exquisite rendering of the exterior, and oftentimes the interior as well. Not only were the front and rear elevations rendered, but also the sides, as well. Mort Lowy, an engineer and builder, who built his daughter and son-in-law's Colcord home in Beverly Hills, said that "the sides were just as important to Gerry, so they were never overlooked."

Clients appreciated seeing exactly what they were paying for. The homes were

Colcord, an extraordinary artist, achieved success early in life by quickly rendering completed drawings of a client's future home.

constructed quickly and efficiently, usually in less than one year. Colcord visited job sites regularly to ensure all was on track. He worked repeatedly with a small group of vendors who knew exactly what he wanted and could produce it flawlessly. Marjorie Greenberg, who built her expansive Beverly Hills Colcord in 1951, recalls: "It was the most pleasurable nine months my husband and I ever spent. There wasn't one problem." Colcord gained a reputation for being honest and fair with everyone. Recommendations from past clients were continually forthcoming, and contractors referred him to their clients as well since Colcord's drawings were so complete that questions seldom needed to be asked.

Colcord had uncanny talent and artistic ability. Ed Warmington, chairman of the board of Warmington Homes (formerly Wm. C. Warmington Co., founded in 1926), told the *Los Angeles Times* in 1983:

> Gerry was a tremendous artist. I saw him design a complete room for people, doing the drawing upside down so they could watch it coming together. He'd say, 'Let's see—how is the library going to look? How are you going to use your furniture? What kind of floor do you want?' He'd draw the room, put in the shelves, design the fireplace, all while drawing upside down. The whole thing would be so perfect that they'd frame it and later hang it in the library, which looked just like the drawing.
>
> Colcord designed some of the most popular homes we ever built. He became so well known for his Pennsylvania Dutch homes and other traditional designs that architectural schools asked him to let them know when one of his homes was nearing completion—so they could take their classes through it.

After an intense day at the drafting table, Colcord loved to socialize and often dropped in on favored clients. Toni Wright, who was sixteen when Colcord designed her family's 1964 Mandeville Canyon home, said, "Mr. Colcord would arrive and begin telling stories—he was a

Colcord poses with his third wife, Virginia, on April 18, 1972.

COLCORD HOME

great mimic. He would have a drink, and then a few more. He would have such a good time that he sometimes forgot about the dinner engagement he had with his wife and she would call trying to locate him."

Besides talent he had charm. Stephanie Stern, who commissioned Colcord to build her home in 1971, recalls that "Gerry was incredibly likable. He always dressed formally, at the least a sport coat, and was very proper. My husband and I had dinner at his home once and we were surprised that it wasn't a 'grand' Colcord, but reflecting now on his lack of pretension, it doesn't surprise me. I repeatedly asked him to sign our house somewhere, but he never did. Rather, he suggested that my children sign the cement floor in the garage."

According to fine artist Shirl Goedike, "Gerry was quiet and, like a typical artist, worked alone. He was pleasant, charming, and sometimes taciturn."

From the beginning, Colcord employed only a small staff—just one or two associates at any given time. When a project was finished he had it photographed for his own portfolio to show future clients. As his fame spread, editors called and were delighted that photos existed—there was that much less to do to produce a finished article. There is no evidence that he ever sought out publicity; nevertheless, he prepared himself for it.

THE 1920s

Colcord began his practice in late 1924 with a Provisional Certificate from the California State Board of Architectural Examiners. He worked as an apprentice to well-known Los Angeles architects including Asa Hudson and John C. Austin.

Price House, begun in 1928 in Beverly Hills, is one of the first houses Colcord built from the ground up. Its style related to the new country houses being designed by architects in Great Britain at the beginning of the twentieth century. They were exploring a contemporary interpretation of the traditional architectural designs of manor houses built from the fifteenth to the nineteenth century,

Price House, 1928, Beverly Hills. One of the first projects Colcord completed from the ground up stands nearly unchanged today.

often expressed by stripping away historic architectural details, leaving only the massing and configuration of the building intact. This approach was explored throughout Europe; in California, San Diego architect Irving Gill reduced the local Spanish Colonial architecture to its essence.

Price House appears to be Colcord's interpretation of the British architects' tenuous Modernism. He has simplified the house while keeping the traditional massing. The wall covering is cement plaster embellished with nothing but a period finish known at the time as "English Cottage." Colcord adopted the splayed wing found in the work of early twentieth century architects such as the Greene brothers and Arthur Kelly. This feature appeared in many of his subsequent projects. Colcord quickly dropped this modernistic approach for unknown reasons. He focused on more popular Tudor and Colonial Revival styles, which he built throughout Beverly Hills, Brentwood, and Pacific Palisades.

THE 1930s

On April 8, 1930, Colcord was granted a State Certificate from the California State Board of Architectural Examiners, Series "C" Number 35, which replaced his Provisional Certificate granted several years earlier. Colcord now signed his architectural documents "Gerard Colcord, C-35."

During the 1930s Colcord designed houses in a diverse range of styles that were highly publicized. In 1931 he accepted a commission from prominent attorney Joseph Horton to build a forty-five thousand dollar French farmhouse in Bel-Air (pages 52–61). Horton House represents Colcord at his best—blending multiple design elements, centuries apart, into a pleasing whole. To this day, it is still the most publicized Colcord project and has appeared in numerous publications.

In the early 1930s Colcord moved out of the family home and married the first of three wives, actress Jeanne Marie Dumas, six years his senior. Theirs was a very social life. They were often mentioned in society columns after attending chic restaurants or parties given by prominent Angelenos. No doubt, the Colcords' society connections contributed to Gerald's success. In the mid-1930s, the couple belonged to the Bel-Air Bay Club and were often seen there, including at a 1936 party themed "Night in Havana."

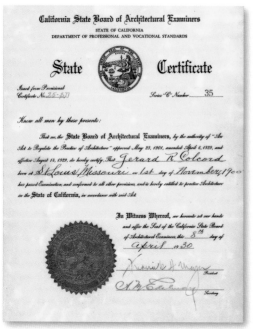

Colcord's certificate from the California State Board of Architectural Examiners was granted in April of 1930.

The Great Depression was omnipresent, but Colcord's business grew nonetheless. Southern California didn't feel the effects of the economic downturn as much as the rest of the United States. Money still flowed in, primarily from the motion-picture industry. Just as important to an architect with a keen eye for detail, craftsmen and artisans from across the United States and Europe moved to Los Angeles to work for the studios, and Colcord could tap them to help manifest his visions.

In 1933, Barker Brothers, an established home furnishings company, asked Colcord on several occasions to conceive "dream house" floor plans and renderings to exhibit in the store. The *Los Angeles Times* often highlighted Colcord's work over other architects' entries and publicized them in the newspaper's "Home Builder's Department" section.

This is most likely how Mr. and Mrs. Philip Chandler learned of him in 1935. Philip, the son of *Los Angeles Times* publisher Harry Chandler, hired Colcord to design his family's 4,500-square-foot French farmhouse-style home in Los Feliz. (Philip's brother Norman, who married Dorothy Buffum, would hire Wallace Neff to design their home a few blocks away.)

Projects were spreading across Southern California. In 1935, Mr. and Mrs. H.I. Sparey commissioned Colcord to build an equestrian estate in Palm Springs at the foot of the San Jacinto mountains. The core is a Monterey Colonial-style featuring the traditional second-floor balcony. Since Colcord's goal was authenticity, albeit liberally interpreted, he used adobe bricks, a board-and-batten second-floor "addition," and the splayed wings he embraced.

In 1938 Colcord designed his first home in the prestigious Los Angeles neighborhood of Hancock

Top: Chandler House, 1935, Los Feliz. Located on a double lot below the Griffith Park Observatory, this French farmhouse was built for *Los Angeles Times* scion Ralph Chandler and his family. *Bottom:* Sparey House, 1935, Palm Springs. This Monterey Colonial-style equestrian estate, built on a generous street-to-street parcel, featured a full basement, quite unusual for the desert. The home was razed.

Top: Hunt House, 1938, Hancock Park, is enhanced with fieldstone, brick, stucco and half-timber construction. Different architectural styles are juxtaposed to give the appearance of a house that was remodeled by progressive generations of a family. *Bottom:* Floor plans for the first and second floors.

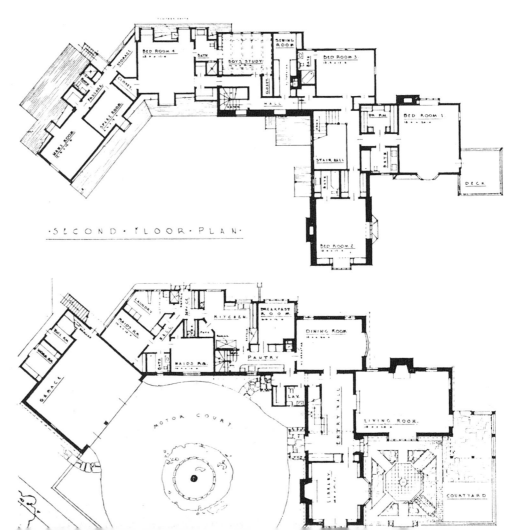

·SECOND·FLOOR·PLAN·

Park, developed in the 1920s by George Allan Hancock. Dr. and Mrs. Verne Hunt commissioned a twenty-room, early sixteenth-century Tudor-style mansion overlooking the Wilshire Country Club. The cost of the home, excluding land, was forty thousand dollars, an extraordinary amount for the time. It's a sublime example of Colcord's trademark: a home that appeared to have evolved over centuries. Colcord built only a few homes in Hancock Park as the area was substantially developed, with few vacant lots available by the time he hit his stride in the mid-1930s. At the end of the decade Colcord moved into a tiny, one-room office at 9538 Brighton Way in Beverly Hills, where he would practice until the end of his career.

Top left: The foyer of Hunt House.
Top right: The two-story entrance hall is the most elaborate room in the house. The surface of the paneled oak walls was smoothed with an adze, an old ax-like tool, to create a period effect.
Bottom: The Tudor-style library features linen-fold oak paneling and a cast-stone fireplace mantle that simulates carved limestone.

THE 1940s

After the bombing of Pearl Harbor on December 7, 1941, residential building slowed dramatically all over the country, including Los Angeles. Men and materials were shipped overseas for the war effort. As a result, Colcord sought other avenues of work, and remained steadily employed during the war years by designing industrial buildings for Douglas Aircraft.

In November 1944, Colcord was granted a divorce from his wife, Jeanne. He agreed to pay her alimony, approximately three hundred fifty dollars per month plus medical expenses, until her sixty-fifth birthday in 1959. He commented to one of his associates that he "always resented sending that check." Days after the divorce was finalized, on November 11, Colcord married Indiana-born Mary Akin Carewe in the Chapel of Westwood Community Church. Mary, forty-three, was the widow of Edwin Carewe, a film director and producer with whom she had three children. Colcord attempted to embrace the children as his own and the newlyweds moved into an existing home on Rexford Drive in Beverly Hills.

Colcord was sometimes asked to design a house's interiors as well. In these cases he often relied on furniture manufacturer Avery Rennick, who had a showroom on Sunset Boulevard—the future site of Scandia restaurant—in West Hollywood. Rennick created high-quality reproductions of American, English and French antiques. Colcord's "Country Colonials" (pages 38–43) with highly asymmetrical floor plans, multiple doors, windows, and numerous fireplaces were challenging to decorate. "Gerry never planned how to furnish one and it was like hell to place furniture," Rennick said to Shirl Goedike.

By the end of the decade, Colcord had become a brand-name architect with work in the pipeline for several years at a time. In 1949, actor Alan Ladd and his manager-wife Sue Carroll decided to build their dream house on a choice Holmby Hills lot. Carroll approached Paramount Pictures and stated that since Ladd was their highest-grossing star, he required a home commensurate with his big-star status, and an interest-free, two-hundred-thousand-dollar loan with which to build it.

The couple hired prominent architect Wallace Neff to design an eight-thousand-square-foot Hawaiian Modern home. But after the foundation was poured and the framing began, the couple had an aesthetic change of heart. They called their builder, Ed Warmington, who chauffeured them around town to look at houses that might appeal more to them. They consistently responded to Colcord's French farmhouses. Warmington phoned Colcord, picked him up and the tour continued. As the four drove through verdant West-

Ladd House, 1949,
Holmby Hills.
Actor Alan Ladd and his wife
Sue Carroll commissioned a
Hawaiian Modern home by
Wallace Neff. Dissatisfied,
the couple hired Colcord and
constructed a one-story French
farmhouse on Neff's original
foundation. Colcord also
designed furniture.
Bottom: He created this desk for
Alan Ladd's son David.

side neighborhoods, Colcord sketched rooflines and elevations, and using the Neff-house footprint, drew preliminary
designs. "That's what we want," the Ladds said after looking at
the drawings he created during the drive.

Their daughter, Alana Ladd Jackson, has fond memories of growing up in their Colcord home. "It was a very happy
place with lots of celebrations. It was the house all the neighborhood kids would visit, especially since we had a swimming
pool. Bing Crosby's kids swam there all the time. Bing was
thrifty and wouldn't install a pool at his house!"

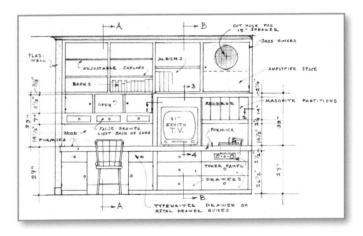

THE 1950s

The 1950s were a sad time for Colcord. After ten years of marriage, his second wife Mary
Carewe, whom he often said was the love of his life, died of a heart attack at age fifty-three
in November 1954. One month later, his mother, Meta, died on Christmas Eve at eighty.
His father had died seven years earlier, so Colcord was alone. Colcord also began having
minor heart attacks that would occur frequently throughout the rest of his life.

With the loss of the two most important women in his life, Colcord consoled
himself with work and designed dozens more Country Colonials throughout Southern

Irvine House,
1941, Stone Canyon.
In an early rendition of Colcord's
Country Colonials, the architect
placed a "window" in the
entrance hall that looks into the
den. This was to simulate a home
had been added onto by a later
owner.

California. Colcord's Early-American form had become so popular that it was the design inspiration for Lucy and Ricky Ricardo's country house on the *I Love Lucy* television series. Set designers relied on readily available design publications (mainly the *Los Angeles Times Home Magazine*) for details when building sets for all the shows produced by Desilu, owned by Lucille Ball and Desi Arnaz. Colcord was at the height of his popularity and was featured, often monthly, in this popular newspaper section.

According to Tom Watson, president of the International *I Love Lucy* Fan Club, Desi Arnaz determined a change of residence was necessary for the storyline, so the Ricardos "moved" to Westport, Connecticut. He felt that since the plots were so zany he wanted the sets, on all of his shows, to be as authentic as possible. For example, water ran in the faucets, switches actually turned lights on and off and when the phone rang, there was an actor on the other end. Guest star Tallulah Bankhead was astonished when she picked up the phone and someone actually spoke to her.

Located at Motion Picture Center in Hollywood (today the home of Ren-Mar Studios), the Connecticut set was so spacious (three times wider than the New York apartment set), that actors required additional dialogue to move them up and down the stage. Producers anticipated a long run, but only thirteen *I Love Lucy* episodes were filmed there by the time the series disbanded in 1957.

Colcord's projects continued to extend beyond Los Angeles. He was commissioned to design Country Colonials in Georgia, Florida, Idaho, Nevada, and Northern California. Evelyn and Edward Schwartz of El Paso, Texas, became clients in 1958. They often vacationed with their children in Santa Monica, and were enchanted with Colcord's designs. "We stopped at one house, knocked on the door, and asked the owner who designed it. That's how we learned about Gerard Colcord," said Edward.

"We phoned Mr. Colcord and made an appointment," he continued. "He was debonair with his cigarette, a tall, good-looking guy. He told us he went to the South of France a lot. He was very classy, very social. Even though he was in his late fifties and we were in our early thirties, we never felt uncomfortable around him. In fact, we quickly called him Gerry. He was easygoing and natural and pleasant. Not pretentious at all, and he could have been with his success level. He only occasionally mentioned celebrity clients.

"He drove us around and toured us through 'his' houses in Chatsworth and Beverly Hills. The owners were as friendly as his houses looked. We were most surprised by his small office. There was one associate working there and plans all over the place. It amazed

us that significant projects came out of such a small office. During our meetings he would tear off a sheet from the vellum roll and start sketching. He said, 'Do you like it this way, or this way?' He was an artist and could draw very quickly."

Colcord visited El Paso just once to site the house. He never saw the house finished, but the Schwartzes sent him many pictures during the nine-month building process. He reduced his fee by one percent since he would not be supervising the construction. "Our builder was extremely complimentary to Colcord because the plans were so complete," Evelyn recalled. As for the fireplace beam, it was made in Los Angeles and sent to El Paso as were the prefabricated marble vanity tops which were superbly crafted.

"We had a generous entrance hall and the living room had a beautiful view of the golf course, which was wonderful. It was just a happy and warm home. We had a large master bedroom, separated from the kids' rooms, and Gerry designed terrific 'his-and-her' bathrooms, kind of a new idea for the 1960s. We wish we still had them! Everyone loved our house and we often heard, 'You have the prettiest house in El Paso.'"

Colcord became known for his heart-tugging family homes that could illustrate a storybook. In fact, his were often called "Storybook style." The essence of his homes and the special features he included for families (doghouses, special playrooms, and children's custom furniture) hint that the concept of family was always on his mind. Ironically, he never had children of his own. The closest he came to his own family was at age forty-four when he married Mary Carewe who already had three children. On his updated post-graduation records from Culver Military Academy, he noted that he had three children, not three stepchildren.

THE 1960s

Colcord, now sixty years old, met and married Virginia Alice Singer. According to those who knew her, his third wife was "a happy-go-lucky lady" twenty-four years younger than Colcord. The couple socialized constantly and particularly loved Tail of the Cock restaurant in West Hollywood. Gladys and Wayne Boynton joined them often at restaurants and the racetrack. When the Boyntons purchased a hilltop lot on which to build their own home, they assumed they would build a trademark Colcord cottage. However, Colcord decided that the view lot dictated a contemporary-style home. "He, of course, was correct and

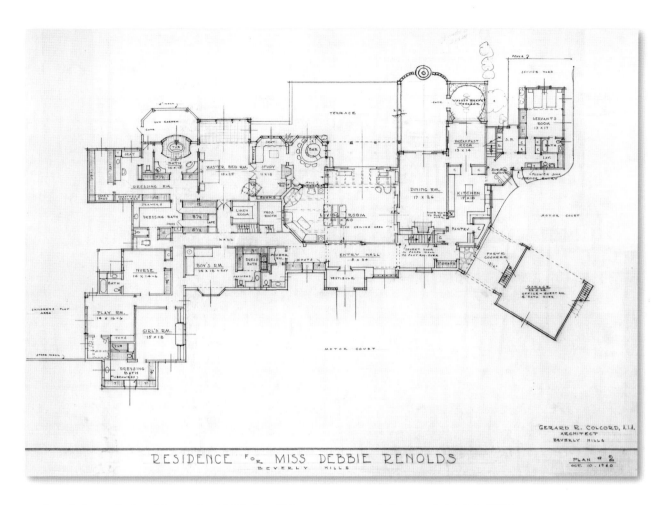

RESIDENCE FOR MISS DEBBIE RENOLDS
BEVERLY HILLS

GERARD R. COLCORD, A.I.A.
ARCHITECT
BEVERLY HILLS

PLAN #2
OCT. 10. 1960

we loved that split-level house," said Gladys. "He even put our infant son's initials 'BB' into the iron gate which is still there today."

In the later part of the decade, Colcord designed a French manor for George and Betty Wing (pages 144–149) overlooking the Pacific Ocean in Palos Verdes Estates. The couple had first interviewed architect Paul Williams who, it turns out, was too ill to consider the commission. Wing House would become one of Colcord's favorite, most time-consuming homes. Every single feature in the almost-seven-thousand-square-foot residence had a working drawing including every door. The contractor, although highly competent, thought "all the drawings were stupid" recalled Betty, and said, "I hope I'm not working when I'm sixty-five like Colcord." Betty snapped, "Artists never retire." And "that was that," she said.

Near the end of the decade Colcord had amassed a significant celebrity clientele due in large part to his stellar professional manner. Hollywood business managers recom-

Colcord developed a significant celebrity clientele due to his extraordinary talent and ethical reputation. This floor plan was created for actress Debbie Reynolds in 1960, but the structure was never built.

mended him because they knew their clients would be honorably cared for.

In the late 1960s, actors Shirley Jones and her husband Jack Cassidy lived in Bel-Air, adjacent to Harris House (pages 110–115). Shirley says that "with three young sons to raise, we decided to move to Beverly Hills because of the school system, which had a great reputation. Jack loved to build things in his garage workshop, and he always had an interest in architecture. He dreamed about living in a home created by either Robert Byrd or Gerard Colcord."

The couple looked at many houses and finally bought a spacious Colcord Colonial Revival-style home in Beverly Hills which had been built for a couple who liked to entertain. "I recall the Realtor telling us about the famous 'Colcord Beam' in the family room fireplace," says Shirley. "We loved that house!" All was calm and peaceful until the *The Partridge Family* appeared on television, starring Shirley and her stepson David Cassidy. "Our doorbell rang about every fifteen minutes," says Ryan Cassidy, the youngest Cassidy son, now a talented set decorator. Shirley says that her second husband, Marty Ingels, finally put a sign near the front door which said, "No Fans, Please."

Above: Located on Rodeo Drive during the 1960s through 1970s, the Swiss Café was designed by Colcord in his classic rural Tudor vernacular.
Opposite top: Built above the Pacific Ocean in 1974 on a prized Palos Verdes Estates parcel, O'Reilly House enchants all who drive by its French-manor façade.
Opposite bottom: Marianna Reilly saved every document related to her home's construction, including a personal letter from Colcord in 1973.

THE 1970s

In 1970, Elizabeth (Liza) Tversiloy Kent joined the firm as Colcord's last architectural associate, previously having worked for popular Beverly Hills architect Ted Grenzbach. The German-born Kent was exacting and highly skilled, a perfect complement to Colcord who was just as detail-oriented. They shared the small office which Colcord had rented since the late 1930s in Beverly Hills.

In 1974, Colcord had to have a pacemaker implanted in his chest and was physically slowing. However, with Kent in place, the office still accepted significant commissions

throughout Southern California and as far away as Pensacola, Florida, and Bellevue, Washington, where a thirty-thousand-square-foot Colcord-designed home was being constructed.

Colcord was backlogged with commissions but when charming clients called he rarely turned them down. Upon seeing Wing House completed (pages 144–149), Mrs. Arthur Reilly knew she wanted a French-style home for the prize ocean-view lot she and her first husband Bob O'Reilly owned. "My husband was in commercial real estate and asked his architect, who created warehouses, to design the house," says Marianna Reilly. "However, the plans really didn't turn out that well! So, I contacted Betty Wing and inquired about her architect. She quickly replied with the most gracious note about her home and its architect, Gerard Colcord.

"I immediately called Mr. Colcord's office to make an appointment. In the kindest way possible he said he just couldn't accept any more work at the moment. I said, 'But couldn't you just take a look at the plans and salvage the unsalvageable?' He must have taken pity on me since he scheduled time for me to visit his office the very next day. We always got along well and the home did turn out beautifully. And that's the reason I'm still here after thirty-four years!"

In the mid-1970s, real-estate developer Bill Lusk, who founded the Lusk Center for Real Estate Development at the University of Southern California and lived in a Colcord house in Newport Beach, hired Colcord for a development he was considering. Plans were drawn, but due to the expense of hiring expert craftsmen, and the extraordinary cost of the homes themselves, he decided not to proceed. "Colcord was one of the finest architects I ever worked with," Lusk noted.

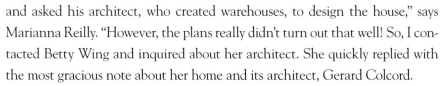

Gerard R. Colcord
Architect
275-3789
9538 Brighton Way
Beverly Hills, California 90210

Dear Mrs. O'Reilly,

Enclosed is a print of Sheet #1, the Plot Plan you requested. Some how it did not get in with the plans I gave you.

I am enclosing a bill of $13.43 for the last 3 sets of plans you requested. I hate to add to your expense, but I have had 12 full sets printed to date not counting the last 3. I usually furnish 8 or 10 sets so you can see they amount to quite a bit for all the extra sets required during a year.

Regards
Gerry Colcord

THE 1980s

Health issues took their toll. Colcord suffered from congestive heart failure, and although still focused on his work, his stamina was waning. In 1979, he started work on a nine-thousand-square-foot Tudor-style home in Pacific Palisades for Mary and Dana Martin. He created an elaborate set of blueprints with his signature trademarks but in a short time he could only walk up the driveway far enough to verify the optimal siting of the house. He never visited that house again, relying on Kent to oversee construction.

In the early 1980s, actor Harrison Ford purchased a 1951 Colonial Revival-style Colcord in Brentwood after having admired Connie Wald's home several years earlier (pages 104–109). Ford met three times with Colcord, and the actor says he quickly developed solid respect and admiration for the architect. "Since the house is in the hills we decided to add a second story to take full advantage of the view. Liza Kent was a major part of the project as Gerry was quite ill at the time. I have tremendous affection for her. While we were working together she would often say, in her thick German accent, 'No limit for better.' That became my motto for life."

In late 1983, Colcord checked himself into a hospital near his Encino home suffering from heart pains. With Kent's assistance, he returned home briefly; however, in January 1984, he was admitted to Cedars-Sinai Medical Center in Los Angeles. He died on February 19, 1984, of cardio-pulmonary arrest and was cremated.

Colcord's widow held a memorial service at Westwood Village Mortuary. Only a small group of friends and associates attended. The *Los Angeles Times* simply issued a death notice. An obituary never appeared.

Kent continued to run the firm under the name of Colcord-Kent; the company

After Colcord's death in 1984, actor Harrison Ford would fly Liza Kent, Colcord's architectural associate, to his West Los Angeles residence to complete the extensive project.

operated until 1989 when Kent closed the office and moved near San Diego.

Of the nearly four hundred homes Colcord designed, most have been time-honored and some have been sympathetically altered (kitchens and bathrooms for the most part). Only about a dozen have been torn down. Existing houses are valued at approximately nine hundred dollars per square foot, according to 2007 sales figures. His homes were extremely well built and often contained three thousand square feet or more, so luckily for those who love them, tearing them down is not economically practical.

Sad exceptions occur. In 2007, an enchanting Colonial Revival farmhouse was listed for sale. Built in 1941 on a spacious lot, the Colcord house was quickly in escrow with a couple who planned to carefully enlarge the home for their family. When they realized that too much work would be necessary, they withdrew the offer. Purchased by a developer, it was immediately bulldozed. But the decimated Colcord Home is the exception, not by any means the rule.

Based upon interviews with people who knew him, it is clear that Colcord was an artist who loved his work so much that personal affluence wasn't particularly meaningful. His only luxuries were wearing fine clothes, patronizing chic restaurants and nightclubs, and owning a boat. During the last part of his life, he lived rent-free in a Colcord house on Woodvale Avenue in the Royal Oaks neighborhood of Encino. The owner could not pay Colcord for services related to a long-term development project, so the house was offered to pay off the debt.

Colcord homes inspire loyalty. They don't come onto the market that often, but when they do, they are often transferred or sold to family members. In many cases, residents maintain special "Colcord Boxes" stored in attics or garages that contain blueprints, renderings and magazines in which their homes had appeared. Several homeowners have designed special stationery bearing photos or renderings of the façade. Families preserve the memories of their Colcord homes. And if they are lucky enough, they preserve the home itself.

Colcord Home came to fruition only because his architectural associate Liza Kent had the common sense and foresight to save his archives. Her decision will enable thousands of residential architecture lovers to learn about the man who has enriched their drives past some the loveliest homes in Los Angeles. Perhaps this book will inspire design practitioners to faithfully interpret Colcord's spirit when they remodel his houses or create structures to become family homes that both delight and stand the test of time.

Carol & Art Hurt had their 1970 Spanish hacienda memorialized by painter by Joel Phillips to create personalized stationery.

Bell House, 1949, Bel-Air.
Mr. & Mrs. Godfrey Bell,
relatives of Bel-Air developer
Alfonso Bell, commissioned
Colcord to build the couple's
residence on a prime hilltop
site. In typical Colcord fashion,
the façades were rendered
simultaneously with the
development of the floor plan.

COLCORD'S COUNTRY COLONIALS

After World War II ended, Colcord's signature genre of Country Colonials emerged. The
United States had been victorious in the war, and new houses reflected an expansive mood
with larger, traditional, American-style homes built on spacious building sites, often in
newly developed tracts in hilly regions. These homes were often one- to one-and-a-half-

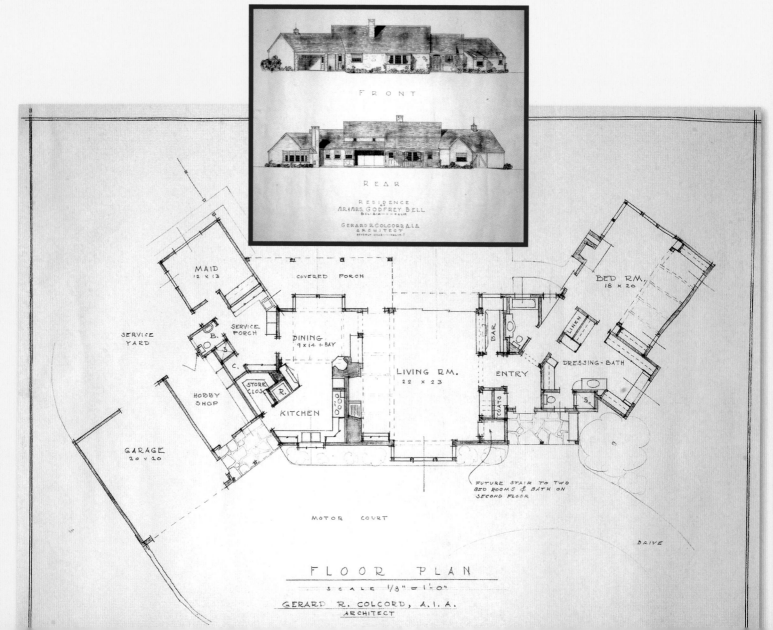

story Colonial Revival-style houses. In Colcord's hands these homes took on picturesque qualities with multiple splayed wings and a nostalgic combination of varied materials. Recognizable trademarks included:

Exterior

- A main, one- to one-and-a-half-story core with multiple splayed wings

- Varying sizes of multi-paned windows

- Clapboard, fieldstone, brick, board-and-batten siding materials

- Paths and terraces of fieldstone or other irregularly laid stones

- Brick and flagstone chimneys which were stone-capped to hide the spark arrestors

- A simulated hayloft over the garage accessed by an outdoor staircase

- A built-in bench at the front door

- A French cock weathervane, a gift to clients, which was handcrafted by a wrought-iron specialist in downtown Los Angeles.

Left: The long driveway at Bell House introduces visitors to the home in stages.
Right: The charming entrance features typical Colcord trademarks: a built-in bench and multi-paned windows.

Colcord embraced modern appliances and simply incorporated his signature brickwork around them. The signature Dutch door features wrought-iron hardware.

Interior

- Exposed rough-hewn wooden beams for ceilings and walls, polished to a rich, lustrous glow in an elaborate, twelve-step process

- Random width, peg-and-groove floors

- Ceilings and walls of hand-textured plaster

- Kitchens with up-to-date appliances with brick surrounds and specific spice and spoon racks

- Spaces which served dual purposes. A powder room with a comfortable sofa that, by night, transformed into a bathtub for overnight guests by removing the cushion.

- Dutch doors

- Multiple fireplaces with the famous "Colcord Beam." What appears to be a wooden beam over the fireplace opening is actually cement and often fools experts, unaware of this design feature. In the 1950s, two Italian mutes constructed most of the beams. Working strictly in secret (other workers were banned from the worksite), they cast a cement block of the appropriate size and, after it cured, applied a coat of cement veneer and quickly "sculpted" tree bark, knotholes and wood grain (using a sandblasted board to imprint texture). After it was set, they applied multiple layers of stain, varnish and paint to simulate the color of an actual hand-hewn log.

Left: Living room looking at the walk-in fireplace with the "Colcord Beam." The large opening is a buffet counter with "guillotine door" to close off the pass-through.
Right: The view into the kitchen past a raised fireplace facing the breakfast room.

The spacious master bedroom with
peg-and-groove floors incorporates an
alcove for the bed that creates a cozy
sleeping area.

By day, this powder room provides guests with an intimate resting spot. By night, the space converts into a full bath when the seat cushion is removed to reveal a bathtub.

TRIPPET HOUSE
Pacific Palisades, 1930

Below: Trippet House, 1930
Opposite: Trippet House, 2006

Trippet House is a fully developed, sophisticated design that invokes a rural French farm complex; a traditional rectangular structure organized around a central courtyard. Like many residences Colcord designed, the architecture had been modified to accommodate the practical demands of twentieth-century Southern California living.

Colcord was only twenty-nine years old when he designed this estate for Mr. and Mrs. Oscar A. Trippet, Jr. Oscar, a prominent civic leader and avid sportsman, owned significant land parcels with his parents. His father, Oscar Sr., a U.S. District Court judge, purchased a family retreat that his mother, Cora, named *Rancho Las Lomas Celestiales* (Heavenly Hills Ranch) in 1917. She hired architect Sumner Spaulding to construct several ranch buildings and today it's known as Trippet Ranch, the centerpiece of Topanga State Park.

Colcord, like many architects of the 1920s and 1930s, found much inspiration from buildings located in the Normandy region in France; Trippet House is representative. The high-pitched hip roof at the fulcrum is the dramatic focal point of the composition and the "kick" at the bottom of the roof, called a coyau (to divert water), reflects a regional characteristic. The gable roofs on the wings, the shed roofs, and hip roofs on the dormers are fundamental to country French architecture.

Rough fieldstone masonry veneer exemplifies the picturesque quality of Trippet House. A massive masonry wall with no window openings facing the street emphasizes the solidity of farm buildings that were designed to be protective. A large-scale projecting fireplace on the street façade told passersby that the house contained a noteworthy provincial fireplace where *pot au feu* was cooking on the hearth. If strictly authentic, the fireplace would have projected into the room rather than outside the exterior wall.

Colcord often modified traditional details. For example, the steel-casement windows in Trippet House, for instance, were generally found only in the most expensive residences—not farmhouses and dependencies which Trippet House mimics. Even the proportions of the thin steel-framed windows are quite different from the heavier wood-framed casement windows found in a French farmhouse. Typically, the roof would have been covered with slate or red clay pantiles. The wood shingles are a uniquely American roof material that replaced the more traditional slate or tiles favored in Europe. An abundant and seemingly endless supply of wood in America was an inexpensive substitute for the more expensive roofing materials used in France.

The home's second owner, Dr. Ernest C. Fishbaugh, was a prominent physician who had tended to the oil-rich Doheny family, owners of Greystone, a forty-six-thousand-square-foot Tudor-style mansion in Beverly Hills. In February 1929, gunshots rang out and thirty-six-year-old Edward "Ned" Doheny and his male secretary, Theodore Hugh Plunkett, lay dead. The family first called Dr. Fishbaugh to the crime scene. When police arrived, the doctor said he hadn't touched the crime scene; later he admitted that he moved Mr. Doheny's body in order to revive him, but others suspected

1930 Commissioned by Mr. & Mrs. Oscar A. Trippet, Jr.
1948 Granted to Hortense Darby & Ernest C. Fishbaugh
1970 Granted to Security Pacific National Bank & George A. Forde, Co-Trustees
1975 Granted to UCLA Foundation
1976 Granted to Ruth N. & William R. Poulton
1982 Granted to Sandra & John R. Borawski
1986 Granted to Iva P. & Browne Greene
1995 Granted to Cathleen & Leonard Waronker
2005 Granted to Amy L. and Robert F. Perille

4,976 square feet; 20,865-square-foot lot
4 bedrooms; 4 bathrooms
1930 building-permit valuation, $25,000; excludes land cost
Builder: Charles Gardner
1930 photography: The Mott Studios
2006 photography: Mary E. Nichols

that he tidied things up to try to avoid any whiff of scandal.

The current owners, Bob and Amy Perille, were drawn to the architecture of Trippet House because it reminded them of their previous Tudor-style residence, a former consulate in Evanston, Illinois. They purchased the Pacific Palisades home from a music executive and found the interiors to be elaborately decorated. Designer Kathryn Waltzer simply "un-decorated" the house and soon after added a pool and outdoor dining complex. The designer notes, "I knew about Colcord when I began the project and tried to intuit how he might have made additions over the years. It is such a beautiful property and my goal was to honor that."

The formal dining room photographed in 1930 (top) contrasts with the more relaxed room in 2006, with no draperies and polished hardwood floors.

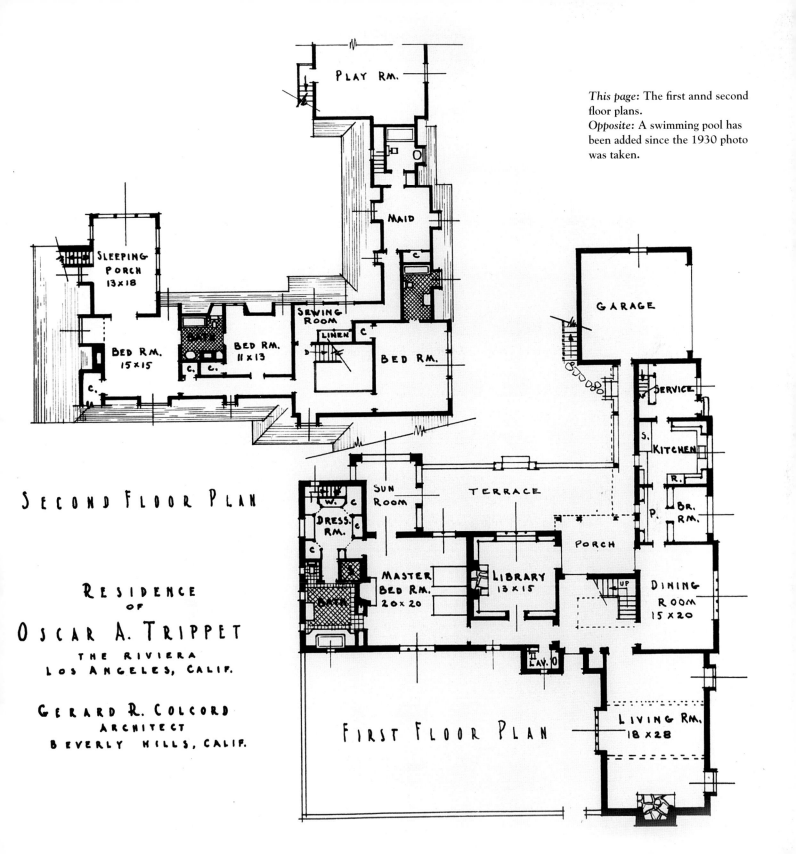

PLAY RM.

This page: The first annd second floor plans.
Opposite: A swimming pool has been added since the 1930 photo was taken.

SLEEPING PORCH 13×18

MAID

c

BED RM. 15×15

SEWING ROOM

BED RM. 11×13

LINEN

c

D

BED RM.

c

c.

GARAGE

SERVICE

S.

KITCHEN

R.

P.

BR. RM.

SECOND FLOOR PLAN

W. c

DRESS. RM.

c

SUN ROOM

TERRACE

c

BATH

MASTER BED RM. 20×20

LIBRARY 13×15

PORCH

UP

DINING ROOM 15×20

RESIDENCE OF OSCAR A. TRIPPET
THE RIVIERA LOS ANGELES, CALIF.

GERARD R. COLCORD
ARCHITECT BEVERLY HILLS, CALIF.

LAV.

FIRST FLOOR PLAN

LIVING RM. 18×28

HORTON HOUSE
Bel-Air, 1932

Horton House incorporates a multitude of architectural styles and is the most frequently published home Colcord designed.

During the second year of the Great Depression, Colcord received another significant commission. He was asked to design an even larger French farmhouse than Trippet House (pages 44–51) one year earlier, for Joseph Kurtz Horton, a prominent and highly respected attorney, and his wife Adele. Their elegant home was one of the first homes built in Bel-Air Estates, founded in 1925.

It was to be one of Colcord's last French farmhouses, and certainly one of his most alluring, though Colcord simply referred to it as "typical of those" found in the Brittany region of France. When the multi-gabled mansion was owned by comedian Bob Newhart and appeared in a 1975 edition of the *Los Angeles Times Home Magazine*, the article noted its "beguiling storybook façade."

Colcord took more design license with Horton House by adding fanciful ornamentation, including additional exposed timbers, moldings and windows, not to mention increased square footage. Individual details were drawn from the sixteenth to twentieth centuries, and architectural elements were interpreted from medieval farm buildings, farmhouses and other agricultural structures found in France and England.

A painterly composition of brick on the street façade is made lively by a series of architectural devices that again bear little relationship to their origins. "Cruck construction," one of a pair of curved timbers forming a principal support of a roof, was generally reserved to support roofs that spanned large open spaces in massive medieval English barns. Here, a miniature cruck frame supports the projecting entrance porch roof.

The house also features a series of gothic arches on the first-floor façade that are meant to simulate openings that had been filled in as the building evolved. Gothic arches were generally used for ecclesiastic buildings and housed stained-glass windows to illuminate the interior of the church. The small area of half-timber construction above these arches on the second floor is primarily decorative rather than structural; this device recalls significant late-medieval barns rather than a residence.

Two small second-floor dormers, often found in third-floor attic spaces, project over the front porch—these windows allow light into the second-floor stair landing. Immedi-

ately next to these dormers are two raised-style dormers (a twentieth-century solution to increase interior headroom) that simulate a later addition to the main structure. The multi-colored slate roof is particularly ingenious, creating the appearance of a weathered roof that has been patched over time.

"Daddy loved beautiful homes and prestigious addresses," says Jo Haldeman, the eldest of three Horton daughters, "and Mother loved to decorate them." Since Horton House was one of the first properties built in the area, Jo would pull her little sister in a wagon across the road (Sunset Boulevard) to play in the surrounding fields—now the UCLA campus.

At least once a month the home was a backdrop for imaginative parties. Often, the family would barbeque around the newly-added pool—a highly unusual amenity in the 1930s, and after dinner guests enjoyed badminton.

In 1934, Mrs. Horton suddenly felt she was ready to deliver daughter number three in the master bathroom. Jo recalls that "Mother yelled for Daddy to get help, and our next-door neighbor, Gladys Beltzer, quickly appeared. All turned out well and my sister arrived safe and sound. Mrs. Beltzer, a famous decorator, and her daughter, actress Loretta Young, lived together. A few years later, Loretta's daughter Judy would become our playmate.

"Daddy often remarked how proud he was to own a Colcord home, but in 1945 he sold the property because gas was rationed. We moved to Linden Drive in Beverly Hills so he could walk to the Red Car station and commute downtown to his office."

Over the years the estate has been extensively altered by its progression of residents.

1931 Commissioned by Adele Ward & Joseph Kurtz Horton
1945 Granted to Raye Becker Fishel
1956 Granted to Virginia W. & Lewis (Peter) W. Douglas, Jr.
1958 Granted to Jean W. & C. James Coberly
1963 Granted to Rita K. & Seymour G. Farber
1965 Granted to Barbara & Milton Taubman
1971 Granted to Jacquelyn C. &
      Andrew Jerrold (Jerry) Perenchio
1973 Granted to Virginia & George R. (Bob) Newhart
1992 Granted to Deidre Hall & Stephen T. Sohmer
2006 Granted to Beverly Hills Property Holdings IV, LLC

6,825 square feet; 25,997-square-foot lot
5 bedrooms; 9 bathrooms
1932 acquisition cost: $45,000
Builder: Wm. C. Warmington
Photography: W. P. Woodcock

Left: A close-up looking past the dining room's alcove window, the loggia and into the den's side window.
Opposite: The rear elevations are just as important as the front, a typical Colcord trademark. This image was taken from Sunset Boulevard.

Left: Ginnie Newhart, who spent nineteen years in this home, especially loved to decorate for the holidays and hosted countless family dinners and special occasions. The den, which overlooks the swimming pool, was a favorite spot for the Newhart family. *Opposite*: The master bathroom overlooks West Los Angeles and the Pacific Ocean through leaded-glass windows.

Above: Kitchens were areas often relegated to servants prior to World War II, but even so, Colcord continued his fanciful details, including brightly colored tiles on the backsplash and countertops.

Opposite: The kitchen stove was brand new; Colcord removed the legs and placed it on a raised hearth with a faux oven opening below.

RYAN HOUSE
STONE CANYON, 1933

Below: The back of Ryan House overlooks an expansive terrace and gardens.
Opposite: The front of Ryan House, set on nearly an acre, harmoniously blends clapboard, white-painted brick and a trellised entry to this Colonial Revival residence.

George Parker Ryan, a contractor who built many of Colcord's early houses, engaged the architect to design his own Bel-Air residence off a lush country road on a one-acre parcel with a running stream. Ryan House was the first of thirteen houses Colcord built on the same street, each representing the styles he favored—American Farmhouse, French Normandy, English Tudor, Spanish Hacienda and Ryan's own Colonial Revival—and all are still standing.

Once again, Colcord interpreted a classic style, Colonial, which became the preferred residential look in the United States during the 1930s. John D. Rockefeller's exhaustive restoration of the eighteenth-century buildings and grounds of Williamsburg, Virginia, was a major influence. At the same time, it became fashionable for residents of large Eastern cities to purchase and restore eighteenth- and early-nineteenth-century houses located in

historic villages and rural areas for use as weekend country retreats.

While new houses were sometimes designed to be historically correct, many were more impressionistic, including Colcord's. Ryan House, like all of his designs, is exceedingly picturesque, and features elements that became hallmarks of the Colonial Revival genre. The large bay window was one such innovation and was typical of shop windows (designed to prominently display goods) that appeared in the early nineteenth century.

The source of the porch-shed-entrance roof supported by a delicate wrought-iron trellis is related to the early-nineteenth-century cast-iron columns found on Regency-style verandahs. Raised dormers are a twentieth-century solution to increase headroom on the second floor while maintaining the appearance of a one-story room with an attic; the attached garage is a variation on the connected barn and outbuildings common to New England farmhouses. The simple picket fence is late-nineteenth-century style; wood fences designed from the late eighteenth to mid-nineteenth centuries tended to be more elaborate and required considerably greater skill to construct.

Inside, the rooms are large, friendly, and filled with classic design details. The simple brick hearth in the living room and spacious hutches in the breakfast room both set the tone for domestic comfort. The upstairs bedrooms incorporate spacious bathrooms and closets (unusual for the time), dormers, pitched ceilings and window seats overlooking mature sycamore trees.

For more than thirty years current resident Marcia Hobbs has loved this property. She states matter of factly: "I was looking for a warm and enveloping house, nothing grand. Every day I appreciate the coziness, the natural light and especially how it's set back on the property. It has been, and continues to be, a wonderful family home."

1933 Commissioned by Clare Clarke & George Parker Ryan
1954 Granted to Charlene & Alfred S. Rosen
1955 Granted to Janice E. & Harry E. Morris
1964 Granted to Carolyn C. Revell
1968 Granted to Margaret T. & Bryon E. Linville
1976 Granted to Marcia Lou & Jeffrey Martin Hobbs
1983 Granted to Marcia Lou Hobbs

2,673 square feet; 1.005-acre lot
3 bedrooms; 4 bathrooms
1933 building-permit valuation, $6,500; excludes land cost
Builder: Ryan Construction Company
1933 photography: W. P. Woodcock

Top: Colcord built in the cupboard at right then simultaneously had a freestanding cupboard made to look as if the breakfast room had evolved over time.
Bottom left: Transitional space between the living and dining rooms features glass shelves at the window and an enclosed cupboard for *objets d'art.*
Bottom right: An upstairs bath includes hand-painted backsplash tiles with contrasting octagonal floor tiles.
Opposite: The living room features a paneled fireplace, complete with wood storage cupboard. Bookshelves line the deeply cushioned window-seat alcove that overlooks a side yard.

UPSHUR HOUSE
SAN MARINO, 1934

Below: The façade of Upshur House features Colcord's ubiquitous "splayed wing" at left. This area housed a chauffeur's apartment directly over the garage and service rooms.
Opposite: The house is on a promontory in San Marino, which on a clear day provides a view of Catalina Island from the rear of the estate.

Amelie McAlister Upshur was a woman of considerable means from New York City, and the West Coast estate Colcord created for her was appropriate to her position in life. In 1940 she bequeathed $262,000 to construct McAlister Auditorium at Tulane University in New Orleans, one of her many philanthropic donations.

Upshur House doesn't follow any specific historical style although it incorporates a number of diverse architectural details loosely related within neo-Regency designs. Examples are a brick-and-clapboard exterior painted white and a Regency-style front porch with a sheet-metal roof supported by nineteenth-century-style wrought-iron posts.

Set on spacious grounds overlooking a private park with views to Catalina, the house is asymmetrical, with the splayed wing found on a number of Colcord projects. The massing and composition of the house are also highly asymmetrical. In contrast, the primary architectural elements used are generally associated with buildings utilizing symmetry to create a formal façade. Colcord freely borrowed architectural details from different periods: the small diamond-pane casement windows and the bay window are found in medieval vernacular architecture, and the "six-over-six" double-hung sash windows and paneled-wood shutters are typical of eighteenth-century Georgian-style houses that evolved from the tradition of Renaissance architecture.

Within, gracious public rooms incorporate a consistent Federal-style design. The entry hall is a model for a beautiful period room. The delicate details of the graceful stair-

With a wide bow window that dominates one wall, the dining room overlooks extensive gardens. Colcord covered the three other walls with a botanical mural to create the effect of dining in a verdant garden year-round.

case, the diminutive keystone above the arched doorway and the refined shapes of the crown molding and baseboard are faithful to the elegant proportions associated with neo-Classical architecture. The historically correct furnishings enhance the architectural details in the room. The wallpaper is typical of the new and expensive wall coverings that became fashionable during this period and the lyre-base table and side chair are also stylistically appropriate for the room.

The elegant paneling in the den is also historically accurate for the neo-Classical period. The receded pilasters, delicate molding on the mantle shelf and the classical urn and swags that adorn the mantle chronicle all the signature features of a Federal-style fireplace mantle. Knotty pine, a wood thought to be inferior, but suddenly in vogue, places the origins of the room in the late 1930s.

Colcord wasn't alone in specifying knotty pine, which became fashionable when people bought and restored eighteenth- and nineteenth-century homes on the East Coast for weekend homes. Owners stripped the woodwork of its paint in the mistaken belief that underneath they would find the beautiful walnut or mahogany paneling found in great English estates. Instead, they uncovered lowly pine with imperfections such as knots, which they carefully polished and presented as the original finish. In the 1960s, scholars and preservationists concluded that nineteenth-century paneling had been painted to hide the poor quality wood to begin with.

Gail and Bob Bardin, the home's current stewards, love the "curve of the staircase when we come in the front door . . . the view to the living room and the library beyond, each framed by an arched doorway . . . the graciousness of the double set of French doors leading out of the living room to the patio . . . and the 'substantial' feeling given by the deep windows throughout the house. The longer we live in the house, the more alive it becomes to us."

1933 Commissioned by Amelie McAlister Upshur
1953 Granted to California Institute of Technology (Cal Tech)
1953 Granted to Virginia L. & Charles E. Hatcher
1957 Granted to Margaret T. & Brooks Gifford
1960 Granted to Margaret J. Cies
1997 Granted to Gail L. & Robert J. Bardin

4,078 square feet; 30,296-square-foot lot
4 bedrooms; 6 bathrooms
1933 building-permit valuation, $24,000; land cost, $8,650
Builder: Wm. C. Warmington
1934 photography: W.P. Woodcock

Right: The elegant foyer features a graceful stairway winding upward to three well-appointed bedroom suites. *Opposite:* The den, paneled in knotty pine, has a secret panel that hides a storage cupboard.

The front porch shows Colcord's skill in blending an array of disparate elements including brick, clapboard, stone and ironwork into a welcoming entrance.

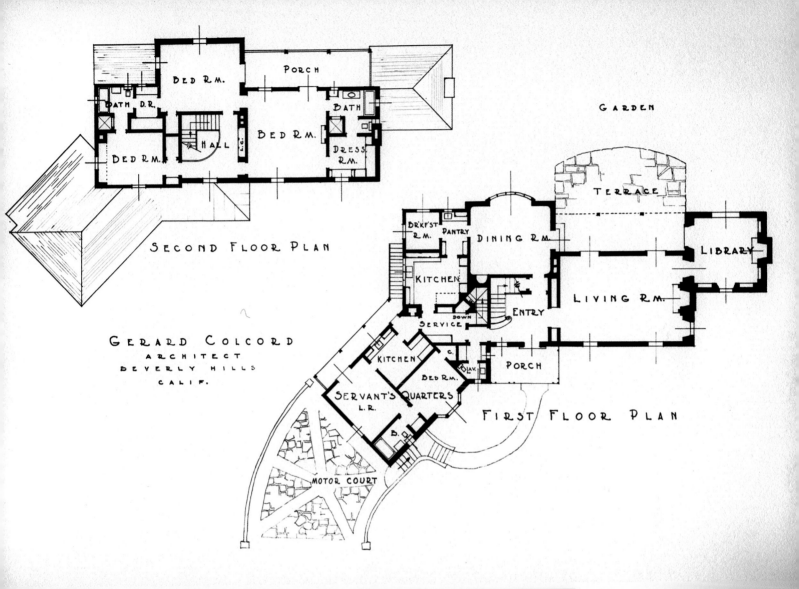

BED RM.

PORCH

BATH D.R.

BED RM.

HALL

BED RM.

BATH

DRESS RM.

SECOND FLOOR PLAN

GERARD COLCORD
ARCHITECT
BEVERLY HILLS
CALIF.

GARDEN

TERRACE

BRKFST RM.

PANTRY

DINING RM.

LIBRARY

KITCHEN

ENTRY

LIVING RM.

SERVICE

DOWN

KITCHEN

C.

LAV.

PORCH

BED RM.

SERVANT'S QUARTERS
L.R.

B.

FIRST FLOOR PLAN

MOTOR COURT

Top: The first and second floor plan of Upshur House. Not shown is a lower-level plan revealing an exquisite array of service rooms including a trunk storage room that is now a sit-down, temperature-controlled wine cellar.
Bottom: The rendered façade of Upshur House.

HORTON HOUSE
Stone Canyon, 1934

Below: The rear terrace of Horton House is adjacent to the master bedroom wing.

Opposite: Colcord was not known for Spanish haciendas yet executed this one adroitly. Here, the hacienda is photographed through the entrance loggia looking into the den's side door.

Attorney William Horton, Sr., and his wife Merrill, didn't look far to find an architect for their new home. Three years earlier, Colcord had designed his brother Joseph's house (pages 52–61), just minutes away. However, the Hortons desired something quite different from his brother's French farmhouse.

Built in a lush, park-like setting, Horton House is one of the few Spanish Colonial Revival houses Colcord designed, and he borrowed ideas from many venues. The layout is a direct descendant of the new, one-story style residences designed by California Arts and Crafts architects between 1900 and 1910. These homes were revolutionary with asymmetrical floor plans, terraces, patios, and wings which splay from a core structure.

Both inside and out, the materials and architectural details at Horton House are associated with Spanish Colonial architecture found in Mexico and California during the

late eighteenth and early nineteenth centuries. Oversized firebricks and/or cast concrete simulate the appearance of adobe bricks. The exterior walls are painted to look like lime wash that was originally applied to walls to protect the adobe from water deterioration and the recessed front porch is a miniature version of the loggias found in California missions. Massive square columns, constructed of the same material as the walls, are articulated with a bold rustic base and capital similar to those found on religious structures. Colcord enhanced the aura of a period arcade with the hand-carved, heavy timber framing of the roof and terra cotta tiles on the floor.

The living room is treated much like the exterior. The exposed roof framing consists of wood-plank sheathing supported by stout hewn rafters and two massive hand-hewn trusses which appear to be the actual structure of the roof rather than the decorative wood framing used in Colcord's Tudor Revival and American Colonial Revival houses. Dominating one wall is a capacious fireplace with a raised hearth constructed of undressed stone blocks and a firebox built with large faux-adobe bricks. An oversized mantle, similar in design and scale to the capitals and bases at the front porch colonnade, frames the firebox. Monumental wrought-iron firedogs, approximately three feet high, embellish the dramatic scale.

The furnishings by Avery Rennick, a prestigious manufacturer of classic reproduction furniture located on Sunset Boulevard in West Hollywood, are in harmony with the over-scaled architectural features.

William Horton, Jr., who was born a few years after construction, and grew up in the house, specifically recalls the home's connection to the natural setting. Famed interior designer John Cottrell visited the hacienda many times when it was rented to Hollywood Regency-style architect Jack Wolf and his adopted son Robert Koch in the early 1960s. Subsequent

1933   Commissioned by Merrill Cowles &
          William Landon Horton, Sr.
1965   Granted to Loretta R. & Ronald F. Howard
1969   Granted to Mary Toshi & Richard D. Walker
1976   Granted to Quincy Jones & Peggy Lipton Jones
1988   Granted to Susan Warchaw & Carl William Robertson

3,000 square feet; 1.670-acre property
5 bedrooms; 4 bathrooms
1934 building-permit valuation, $20,000; excludes land cost
Builder: unknown
1934 photography: W. P. Woodcock

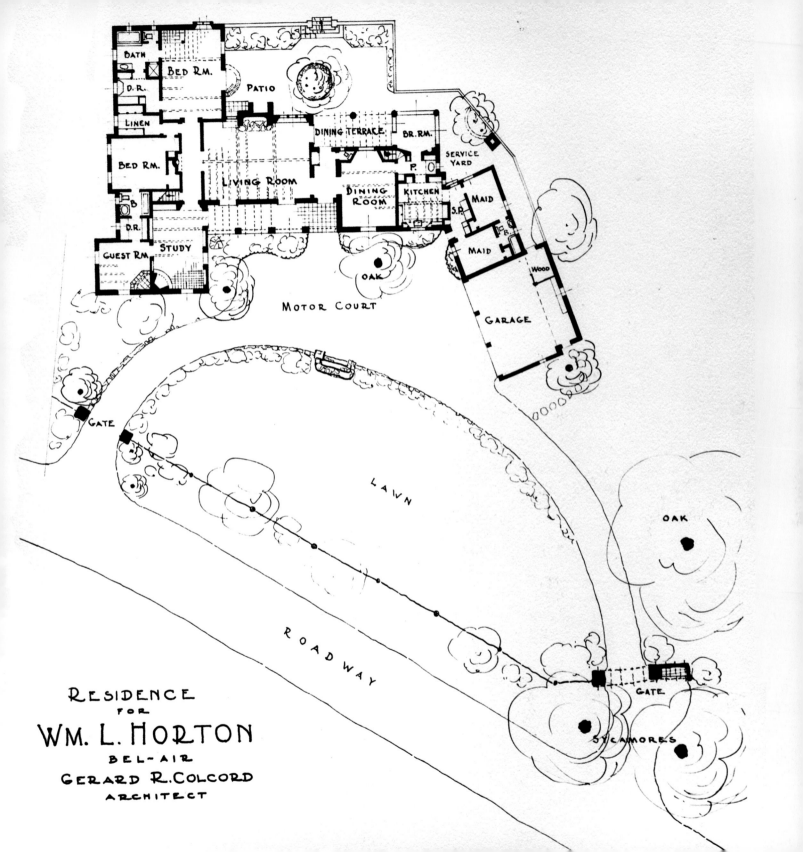

BATH

BED RM.

D.R.

PATIO

LINEN

DINING TERRACE

BR. RM.

SERVICE YARD

BED RM.

LIVING ROOM

KITCHEN

MAID

DINING ROOM

S.P.

B.

D.R.

STUDY

MAID

WOOD

GUEST RM.

OAK

GARAGE

MOTOR COURT

GATE

LAWN

OAK

ROADWAY

RESIDENCE
FOR
WM. L. HORTON
BEL-AIR
GERARD R. COLCORD
ARCHITECT

GATE

SYCAMORES

Avery Rennick decorated the living room anchored by a Chinese red Oriental carpet. The cabinet on the wall to the left of the elongated fireplace housed radio equipment.

owners dramatically altered the home by tripling its size and adding a pool. Cottrell, who honored the structure's simplicity and use of materials from its original state, later designed the interiors for owners Quincy Jones and his wife Peggy Lipton during the late 1970s.

A rear dining terrace with log loggia is reached via the dining room doors.

LOCKE HOUSE
Santa Anita Oaks, Arcadia, 1937

Below: Locke House is still on its original two-acre parcel in the pastoral neighborhood of Santa Anita Oaks near Pasadena. *Opposite:* Patterned after country houses constructed for affluent families on the East Coast, Locke House was featured in the 1998 Academy Award-winning film, *Gods and Monsters.*

While Colcord primarily worked for clients in Beverly Hills and the Westside of Los Angeles, he designed at least six houses in the San Gabriel Valley, including this nearly two-acre estate with its own barn in Arcadia, once serious horse country. Three years before it was built in the foothills of the San Gabriel Mountains, celebrated Santa Anita Park, a racetrack co-owned by movie mogul Hal Roach, opened, drawing the biggest celebrities of the day, including Bing Crosby, Spencer Tracy, Errol Flynn and Al Jolson, all of whom raced their horses there.

Mr. and Mrs. Edmund Locke could have hired any of the eminent Pasadena architects at the time—including Roland E. Coate, Myron Hunt, or Wallace Neff—but Colcord's reputation had spread. He was abundantly skilled to design estates that were at home with the numerous Period Revival-style residences emerging in the area.

Locke House is based upon Federal-style country houses built in the eastern Unit-

The focal point of the entrance hall is an elegant staircase accessing four bedroom suites. Numerous weddings and receptions have been held in this home, says owner Kathy Gormly, who with late husband Donald, reared seven children.

ed States between 1776 and 1820. Named after America's first political party, Federal-style design was derived from Greek and Roman architecture to embody the ideals of Greek democracy and the Roman Republic. The sublime Greek and Roman temples that survived and the secular buildings discovered at Pompeii and Herculaneum in the late eighteenth century provided the detail and formed the basis for neo-Classical architecture.

Although they were modest in size compared to more imposing two-story, Georgian-style country houses, Federal-style details were often much more delicate and refined. Homewood, a Baltimore house built in 1800 for Charles Carroll, a signer of the Declaration of Independence, could well have served as inspiration for Colcord. A striking and unusual feature of Homewood was the decorative detail used to embellish the pediment of the entrance porch—also found on Locke House.

Other prominent features of Homewood appear as well: brick veneer on the walls of the main center block, elongated windows at the first level and small dormers with circular head windows on the second floor. The white painted brick was a popular Los Angeles design choice and is frequently seen on many 1930s Colonial Revival homes built in Southern California.

Elements of Locke House that depart from tradition include turning the two end wings at right angles to the main section of the house, perhaps for property-width considerations; utilizing wood shingles on the walls of the two end wings; and crowning the front door with a Georgian-style broken pediment.

"My late husband Donald bought this house before I even knew about it," says Kathy Gormly, who for the past forty-one years has presided over Locke House. "After my husband told me about his purchase, I was very annoyed. However, he drove me over and I quickly fell in love with the house. Besides being beautiful, it was so nice and big—enough bedrooms and bathrooms for our seven children."

1937	Commissioned by Elizabeth Browne & Edmund Locke
1942	Granted to Thelma G. & Carl E. Baker
1948	Granted to Mary Jo & William D. Voit
1961	Granted to Mary S. & Emory F. Sawyer
1965	Granted to Donald & Ruth Kathy Gormly

6,612 square feet; 1.756-acre property

6 bedrooms; 5 bathrooms

1937 acquisition cost: $37,500; excludes land cost

Builder: Wm. C. Warmington

1937 photography: Maynard L. Parker

The den is a favorite spot for the Gormly family; the door to the right leads to a guest suite.

Kathy speaks glowingly about the dozens of Little League gatherings, church parties, five children's weddings, seven children's wedding receptions and benefits she often hosted at Locke House. Not surprisingly, this elegant and well-maintained home continually attracts the attention of Hollywood location scouts. In fact, front and back façades, pool, and cabana of Locke House played an important role in the 1998 Academy Award-winning movie, *Gods and Monsters*, serving as the residence of movie director James Whale, played by Ian McKellen.

Top: "Many children's counseling sessions have been conducted on the window seat," says Mrs. Gormly. The window seat is to the left of the fireplace in the master bedroom.

Bottom: The Lockes, who commissioned the home, had four girls and two boys. This is one of the two girls' suites.

Above and right: The master bathroom hasn't been changed since it was built. "Why remodel when it's perfect?" asks Mrs. Gormly. The octagonal window is a Colcord trademark, particularly in bathrooms.
Opposite: The excellent flow of the floor plan has easily accommodated hundreds of guests at family get-togethers, parties and fundraisers over the years.

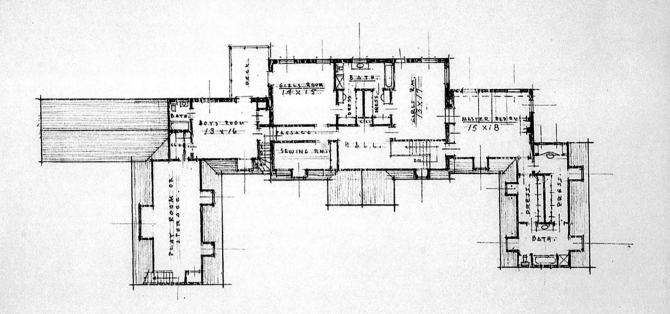

SECOND FLOOR PLAN.

SCALE: 1/16" = 1'-0"

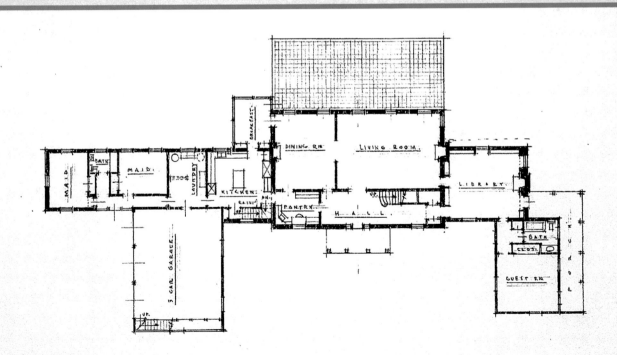

FIRST FLOOR PLAN.

SCALE: 1/16" = 1'-0"

BOGGS HOUSE
Westwood Hills, 1938

Below: The traditional, narrow staircase emanates from the foyer with painted tongue-and-grove paneling and period-correct hardware.
Opposite: Boggs House features a delightful array of Colcord details including the lean-to addition on the left, and a classic Gambrel-style Colonial core. The right-side wing, which looks as though it was a later addition, was designed to look as if the house had evolved over time.

Marking his fourteenth year in practice, Colcord accepted a commission for a three-bedroom house that would measure just over two thousand square feet. Despite the smaller scale, he didn't scrimp on myriad, charming details. In fact, Boggs House, within walking distance of UCLA, boasts some of Colcord's finest design elements, particularly a small open porch with delicate posts that support a gently curved fascia board, which became one of the archtect's trademarks. The small wooden fence placed close to the façade (to create the sense of an intimate dooryard garden), a carriage-light fixture on a turned-wood post, and an informal garden border were all features that reappeared later on larger Colcord houses in even grander neighborhoods.

Boggs House is a replication of a European Gambrel Colonial-style structure featuring architectural details related to modest American residences constructed during the first half of the eighteenth century. The dominant feature, the gambrel roof, was originally created to provide ample headroom on the upper floor in a one-and-a-half-story house. Although this style is usually referred to as Dutch, it was, in fact, a roof form used throughout the colonies and can be seen in Connecticut, New York, Pennsylvania, Maryland, Virginia and the Carolinas. (The gambrel roof was also used on eighteenth-century terrace houses in London where it was termed a "curb roof.")

Also related to these early-eighteenth-century homes are the "six-over-nine" double-hung window sashes; numerous small panes of glass were common features because large sheets of glass were difficult and costly to manufacture. The most common form of glass used between 1710-1760 was "blown glass." A flat circular sheet of glass was

made by rotating a metal punt onto which the molten glass was poured. Square panes were cut from these flat circular sheets but were limited in size by the circumference of the glass plate. The small piece of glass attached to the metal punt was called "bull's eye glass" and was often used in transom windows, such as the one over the front door of Boggs House.

Three small bays on the first and second floors contain casement windows with leaded glass panels. These windows, typical of the seventeenth century, are an anachronism at Boggs House. Since Colcord desired that his houses "tell stories," it's possible that the purpose of these windows was to give the residence the appearance of a late-seventeenth-century house that had been modified in the early eighteenth century by subsequent residents. The same could be said for the lean-to shed "addition" on the left and different roof line—a steep gable with a pitch unrelated to the gambrel and shed roofs—that covers the porch on the right. In any case, borrowing design elements from random centuries was something Colcord would continue to adroitly implement; Boggs House was just the beginning. Style differences created an air of informality as opposed to the strict symmetry found in more expensive, high-style residences.

Historic authenticity never got in Colcord's way, then or in his later houses. The oversized square chimney would appear authentic if it was located in the center of the roof rather than at the side. A chimney of this size and proportion rising through the center of an early-eighteenth-century roof would have indicated that three or four corner fireplaces shared one chimney.

Current owner Marjorie Hansen bought the house from Mr. and Mrs. Charles Manning, and she kept intact many of the touches designed by Annette Manning, an interior decorator. "The Boggses divorced and sold it the Mannings," says Miss Hansen. Charles Manning, professionally known as Charles Knox, a popular radio announcer, developed throat cancer and changed professions, working for then-Senator Richard Nixon in Washington, D.C., and renting out the house until the couple returned to Westwood.

1938   Commissioned by Louise & John D. Boggs
1940   Granted to Annette N. & Charles Knox Manning
1966   Granted to Marjorie Hansen

2,158 square feet; 9,448-square-foot lot
3 bedrooms; 2 baths
1938 building-permit valuation, $7,500; excludes land cost
Builder: unknown
1938 photography: Maynard L. Parker

After moving in, Miss Hansen wanted to replace window shutters at the front of the house, but needed special exterior hooks. She learned who the architect was and called his secretary who gave her his home phone number. "I reached Mr. Colcord and explained the situation. He said, 'Oh, you have one of my smaller houses.' Graciously, he told me about Beverly Hills Hardware where they had exactly what I needed. He was delightful on the telephone."

Miss Hansen is remembered by countless Westside families as the beloved principal of Palisades Elementary School. Hansen says, "My guests always love coming here. I've had sixty-five people for tea to introduce a new principal to the PTA, and every other kind of party you can imagine. I even have special Christmas dishes for holiday parties. When you get to be ninety-two you have stories to tell. I feel so lucky to have found my profession and a grand home where I entertained so many friends, family and colleagues. Everyone has always had a good time here, especially me."

The rear of Boggs House is as detailed as the front. A garage at left is reached via a long loggia.

A dormer window punctuates one wall, creating a charming ceiling angle in one of the guest rooms.

Right: The breakfast room features glass shelves to display colorful glassware. The Dutch door, originally designed to provide ventilation while keeping livestock out of a farmhouse, features a hinged shelf in which to cool freshly baked foods.

Opposite: The kitchen opens into the dining room. The custom-designed spoon rack is another Colcord trademark.

WRIGHT HOUSE
San Marino, 1938

Before the Second World War, affluent Americans frequently turned to England for style and respectability and, during the 1920s, "Stockbroker Tudor," as it was commonly known among newly minted millionaires and their architects, was all the rage. Colcord had designed several dozen Tudors by 1938, and when investment advisor and music professor Dr. Douglas Wright, Jr., called about his two large adjoining parcels in a well-manicured neighborhood in San Marino, next to railroad magnate Henry E. Huntington's 120-acre estate, Colcord was at his best.

Wright House is one of Colcord's most exquisitely detailed English residences, extraordinary inside and out. The living room is probably the finest interior space he ever designed. It is also one of the few with a choir balcony. Dr. and Mrs. Wright often gave recitals there, playing duets on "his-and-her" grand pianos or giving individual performances on the pipe organ.

Left: The back entrance foyer, with leaded clerestory-style windows, and the stair hall introduce exquisite architectural detailing that is almost impossible to reproduce today.
Right: To the left of the living room Tudor-arch fireplace is a secret-door panel, which hides the organ pipes. The floor-to-ceiling window on the right features strips of lead randomly placed to simulate window repairs made over centuries. The ceiling is twenty feet high.
Opposite: The façade of Wright House beguiles all who drive or walk by. Current owners Mary Ann and George Leal have entertained countless guests over thirty-five years of thoughtful stewardship.

The house bears signature features associated with fifteenth-century English manor houses and residences commissioned by the "middling sort," the emerging merchant and professional class in England. The half-timbered and cement-plaster panels simulate the appearance of a timber-frame building with "wattle-and-daub" construction. A mixture of clay, sand and straw, called "daub" was applied between the timbers, or "wattles." The curved diagonal braces are authentic to the period. Colcord used masonry veneer on the one-story wing, and on the second floor as well. This section projects over the ground floor to suggest it was added at a later date.

For variety and interest, the leaded-glass windows are of differing sizes and patterns. The decorative "bargeboard" (boards fastened to the projecting gables of a roof to give them strength and protection from the elements) and finial on the gable end of the roof are typical of the Tudor period. A flat clay-tile roof would have been used in England because of the danger from fires. Wood shingles were commonly used in Southern California since they require a much lighter roof framing system and wood was more plentiful. The engaged double chimneystack simulates chimneys that were crafted in the fifteenth century.

Inside, the elaborate wood-truss framing in the living room is based upon typical roof framing found in late-medieval halls and churches. While the framing members used on the exterior are cosmetic, the framing system in the living room is structurally sound. The Tudor moldings, the knee braces, hammer post and arch brace are elegant replications of period woodwork. The Gothic-arch doorway framing plank doors and the Gothic-arch windows in the entry hall reinforce the historical appearance of a great hall. The choir balcony above the entrance simulates the appearance of a gallery in a church or a space for musicians to entertain guests in the hall of a residence. The irregular panes of glass were designed to imply ancient stained-glass windows that

1937 Commissioned by Ruth L. & Dr. Douglas Wright, Jr.
1943 Granted to Ruth L. Wright
1960 Granted to Jane C. Allen
1967 Granted to Jane C. & Robert Moffatt Allen
1972 Granted to Julian B. & Stephen E. Fife
1976 Granted to Kathleen & Edward J. Templeman
1976 Granted to Mary T. & George D. Leal

4,376 square feet; 29,699-square-foot lot
4 bedrooms; 5 bathrooms
1937 building-permit valuation, $33,444; land cost, $9,000
Builder: unknown
1938 photography: Maynard L. Parker

A massive Tudor-arch fireplace in the den is enveloped by linen-fold oak paneling den. What appears to be a secretary is actually a storage bin for fireplace logs that can be loaded from an outdoor passage.

had been patched over the ages.

At the far end of the room is a fireplace with a simple Tudor arch. The carved paneling surround serves as a portal for the organ music, and disguises a secret panel that accesses the organ pipes. Many of the original furnishings, including hanging lanterns, sideboard and the flagon are typical of the period, and the settee is a good reproduction of a late-seventeenth-century William and Mary piece.

"It was love at first sight when I saw the house," says current resident Mary Ann Leal, who, with her husband George, raised two children here and entertained many friends and groups in the home. The Leals found the property in near-original condition. The only substantive change they have made since moving in more than thirty years ago is a careful update of the kitchen.

Mary Ann continues, "We are often asked by location scouts to film here, one time by the producers who made *Nightmare on Elm Street*. We usually decline since we can't bear the thought of any damage. We love our home!"

Across the reflecting pool, benches flank an outdoor fireplace. Colcord created this conversation spot with warm Pasadena evenings in mind.

BARNETT HOUSE
Beverly Hills, 1939

In the exact center of Beverly Hills is Colcord's most renowned home, a Pennsylvania Dutch-style estate occupied since 1943 by internationally celebrated hostess Connie Wald. She continues to entertain her family and the world of notables who pass though her front door.

Forget the Beverly Hills address, and it's easy to imagine Barnett House set somewhere in the flourishing countryside outside Philadelphia where this eighteenth-century Colonial Revival-style home, often referred to as Pennsylvania Dutch, originated. With its perfect scale and proportions, Barnett House is one of Colcord's finest Colonial Revival homes, the style for which he is best known. It embraces many of Colcord's favorite motifs, preeminently the fieldstone masonry façade.

Colcord was manifestly familiar with the details that comprised historically correct Colonial houses, details that developed and grew. Traditionally, the oldest section of the house was a one-and-a-half story structure with a steep pitched roof that dated from the late seventeenth century—seen here on the second floor with dormers. In the mid-eighteenth century, the largest portion of the house was built—a two-story core to provide more refined public spaces and bedrooms The first structure now functioned specifically as the kitchen wing; this addition appears at Barnett House as the center of the house. As families grew, a third section was often added towards the end of the eighteenth century or beginning of the nineteenth century, seen here on the extreme right.

Barnett House emphasizes other features that frequently appeared in Colcord's Pennsylvania Dutch designs: two wings flanking the main section of the house, a paneled front door painted white; delicate posts supporting the gently curving fascia boards, a glass-and-sheet-metal wall lantern; and a simple, white picket fence to frame the house. Flagstone paving on the sidewalk and porch floor became a popular choice for Colonial Revival houses built in the 1930s and 1940s, yet does not have any historical precedent.

In the Philadelphia region, it was common to protect masonry walls with a coating of lime plaster. However, in Southern California, where severe climate concerns are hardly an issue, Colcord took a decorative approach. On the porch, he coated the stone veneer with cement plaster painted white to simulate an original lime wash, a flourish which accented the home's entrance.

The "twelve-over-eight" double-hung windows on the first floor are typical of generously-sized, mid-eighteenth-century windows, where the upper sash is larger than the lower

Decorator Tom Buckley believes the screening room is one of the most beautiful interior spaces in Los Angeles. Connie's son Robert Wald recalls returning from school one day and casually saying hello to Joanne Woodward, Paul Newman, Marilyn Monroe and Cary Grant, all of whom were enjoying a movie in the family home.

one, while windows with "six-over-six" double-hung sashes were used on the second floor. Colcord also paid correct attention to variations in shutters. Paneled shutters on the first-floor windows were originally meant to be closed at night for security; Venetian-style shutters upstairs allowed for air circulation and privacy due to the fixed louver design. Painting the first- and second-floor shutters in complementary colors, however, was pure Colcord flair.

Four years after it was built, Barnett House was purchased by legendary movie producer Jerry Wald (credits include *Sons and Lovers*, *Mildred Pierce*, *Peyton Place*, *Johnny Belinda*, *From Here to Eternity* and *Key Largo*, among many others) and his elegant wife Connie. Shortly after the couple married, they saw a "For Sale" sign posted and quickly approached the owners, W.B. Barnett, a retired businessman from Pennsylvania, and his wife Minnie. "They became frightened after World War II started, afraid the Japanese were off the coast of Santa Barbara ready to bomb Southern California, which is why they were selling," recalls Connie, a formidable Hollywood hostess who, in 2007, at age ninety-two, was named on *Vanity Fair's* International Best Dressed List.

"Mrs. Barnett didn't like me at first, and thought I was much too young to know anything about this house—I was in my early twenties." Nevertheless, the sale went through and the Barnetts moved to the East Coast. After the war, they returned to Los Angeles and rehired Colcord to build a smaller dream house nearby. "Mrs. Barnett and I became very good friends after she saw I hadn't damaged 'her' house."

The Walds hired Gladys Beltzer, Loretta Young's mother, one of the most fashionable decorators of the day, to help them pull the house together. Belzer organized the rooms in a stylishly traditional manner with fine period antiques, and the décor is nearly unchanged today.

In 1952, when Jerry Wald was at Columbia Studios, the studio offered to build him an at-home screening room, and the Walds first met Colcord. "That room was formerly a lovely morning room, but Mr. Colcord expanded it flawlessly as if it had always been part of the house.

"In 1955, my father died, so my mother came to live with us. I called Mr. Colcord

1939   Commissioned by Minnie & W.B. Barnett
1943   Granted to Connie & Jerry Wald

5,443 square feet; 17,990-square-foot lot
5 bedrooms; 6 bathrooms
1939 building-permit valuation, $20,000; excludes land cost
Builder: unknown
1938 photography: Maynard L. Parker
2008 photography: Mary E. Nichols

Los Angeles decorator Gladys Beltzer furnished the home in the early 1950s and little has changed since. The flawlessly proportioned living room seamlessly blends choice antiques and contemporary art.

back, who added an upstairs 'tree house' apartment. Soon after, he also added a swimming pool and some changing rooms to an existing outdoor pagoda."

One of Connie's closest friends, Audrey Hepburn, always stayed with the couple when she was in town. "One day," remembers Connie, "she was in the garage and laughed, 'Connie, the only thing you have in here is an icebox and a Rolls-Royce.' Mr. Colcord returned and converted the garage into Audrey's guesthouse, which we called Baron's Barn."

Jerry Wald died of a heart attack at age fifty in 1962, but Connie continued to open her home to Hollywood stars and notables. She remembers that Harrison Ford was so taken with the house that he subsequently bought his own Colcord dwelling in Brentwood. "He was enchanted when he saw the huge fireplace.

"So many friends and so many wonderful memories—Jimmy Stewart, who visited often, would say, 'Connie, your home is marinated with life.' Everyone who visits is always welcomed by the Colcord magic of loving and lasting design."

The den is filled with memorabilia from a distinguished life. Guest Harrison Ford was once so impressed with the massive fireplace and the famed "Colcord Beam" that he later purchased a Colcord home in Brentwood for himself.

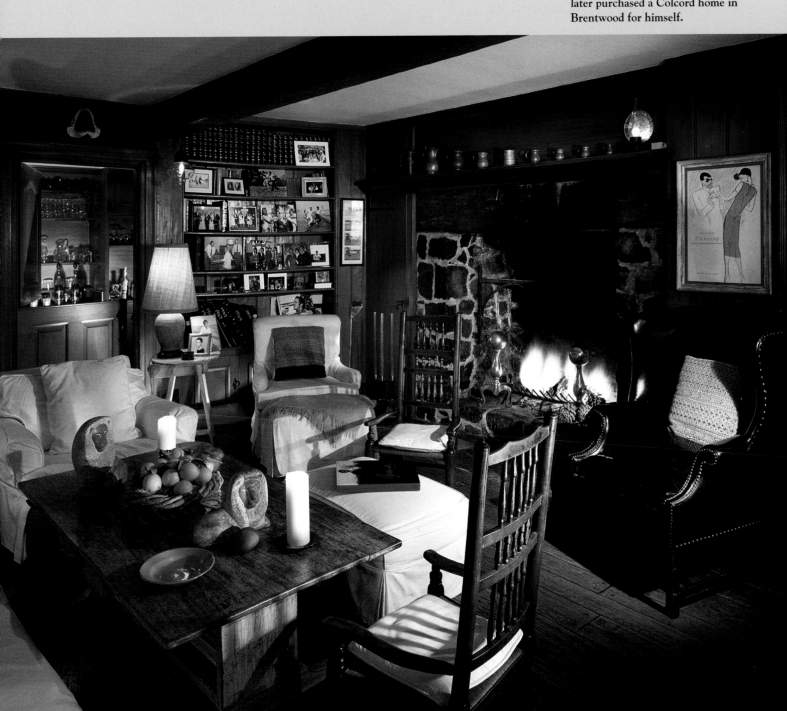

HARRIS HOUSE
Bel-Air, 1940

Below: **Mrs. John Wesley Harris commissioned Harris House at a total cost of $110,000. Sited on a wide, one-acre parcel minutes from the Hotel Bel-Air, celebrity occupants later included entertainers Dean Martin, Tom Jones and Nicolas Cage.** *Opposite:* **The motor court can be seen through the entrance gate. Harris House was Colcord's largest and most opulent home at the time. On the tower, the diamond pattern brickwork is known as "diapering."**

A prime residential parcel in Bel-Air, originally owned by Robert E. Gross, president of Lockheed Aircraft Corporation, provided the setting for what is probably Colcord's most impressive and richly detailed house, a baronial English Tudor.

When Harris House was first built, grand English Tudors were somewhat out of step with the architectural taste of the time. Producers David O. Selznick and Jack Warner had recently both commissioned architect Roland E. Coate to build their Colonial Revival mansions in Beverly Hills, and architect Paul Williams had designed the Beverly Hills headquarters of the powerful Music Corporation of America in a similar Colonial Revival manner. Still, grand English Tudors were a preferred style for institutions, colleges and occasionally mansions for the very rich. Mrs. Harris, widow of a wealthy land developer who developed parts of Westwood, fits into the last category.

By the late 1930s, Colcord had designed many Tudor Revival houses, which were modeled after modest urban and rural residences from the fifteenth and early sixteenth

centuries. Harris House is based upon the significantly grander manor houses from the period, and reflects the transition in British architecture that occurred when Henry VII consolidated the power of the state under one ruler. Heretofore, the need for defensible residences required buildings to have impenetrable walls and rooms that faced inward to a courtyard—bastions from which to fight the enemy.

The creation of an orderly state allowed the ruling class to safely construct homes that did not have to turn inward for safety. This development, along with the advanced technology in glass manufacturing, radically altered the type of house that was safe to inhabit in the countryside. The most notable change to British residences was the enthusiasm for windows, so the masonry walls of country houses were made as limited as possible to allow for great expanses of glass. "Hardwick Hall, more window than wall," went a popular English rhyme about the ultimate house built for Bess of Hardwick to entertain the Royal House on their progressions through the countryside.

In true Colcord fashion, the design of Harris House appeared to have its own storyboard—the central tower and entrance hints that they are the remains of a castle that has been encapsulated by an expanded Tudor residence. The square tower, the focal point of Harris House, is typical of the vestigial battlement towers that were the primary feature of thirteenth- and fourteenth-century castles, although the crenellation has been replaced by decorative brickwork and the small slit openings have been replaced by a set of ribbon windows. The Gothic buttresses that articulate the walls on either side of the main entrance express the evolution of the structure. The decorative brickwork on the house also represents a change in the use of building materials during the Tudor period. Previously, stone masonry had been the traditional building material for

October 1938	Commissioned by Mrs. John Wesley Harris
June 1964	Granted to the University of Southern California (USC)
June 1964	Granted to Joanne & Stanley Stalford
April 1968	Granted to Eugenia Clair & Ivan Smith
October 1972	Granted to Dean Martin
June 1976	Granted to Melinda E. & Thomas (Tom) Jones Woodward
March 1998	Granted to Nicolas Cage

11,817 square feet; 43,116-square-foot lot
9 bedrooms; 9 bathrooms
1939 building-permit valuation, $85,000; land cost, $25,000
Builder: Wm. C. Warmington
1940 photography: Maynard L. Parker

fortified structures because it was impenetrable and difficult to dismantle.

Brick masonry walls were a much lighter form of construction. Bricks took less time to manufacture and building with them was easier and faster than quarrying and setting stone. Brick also lent itself to creating decorative designs to embellish the walls. The quilted or "diapering" pattern on the tower is representative of some of the geometric designs that became popular—and possible.

Inside, the great Louis XV staircase and immense 1930s art deco or Moderne windows in the entrance hall are in step with the capricious character of twentieth-century eclectic architecture—and are a departure for Colcord, whose interiors usually related to the exterior architectural theme. Not to be forgotten—it was possible for owners to pick and choose the fantasy they wished to inhabit.

Over time Harris House has been home to a number of celebrities: Dean Martin, Tom Jones and as of 1998, Nicolas Cage. In 1974, Dean Martin asked Colcord and his associate Liza Kent to add a $313,000 entertainment complex, with interiors by Laura Church Mako. The 2,500-square-foot addition accommodated a foyer, curtained stage and movie screen, projection room, sunken wet bar, large fireplace, two marble baths, two dressing rooms and a children's playroom in the tower.

Above: A marble fireplace nearly six feet tall is the focal point of the living room. *Opposite:* The formal dining room features period-correct furnishings and a hand-cast plaster ceiling.

IRVINE HOUSE
STONE CANYON, 1941

Below: Irvine House is the quintessential storybook cottage that delights all who visit.
Opposite: The formal dining room features a corner-fireplace. Another Colcord trademark is the exquisite paneling and storage cupboards with hand-forged "L & H" hinges.

In the 1860s James Irvine bought an interest in three major Southern California ranchos and his holdings were the genesis of the Irvine Company. The city of Irvine in Orange County is located on lands once owned by the Irvine family. A descendent of the family purchased a far smaller parcel in a choice picturesque area of old Bel-Air to build a modest-yet-charming house designed by Colcord in the eighteenth-century Pennsylvania Dutch-style that Colcord masterfully adapted with a nod to the Southern California lifestyle.

Intended to resemble a small stone house with numerous additions, the core section mirrors a one-room brick or stone farmhouse built by early Swedish, German, Moravian or English settlers at the end of the seventeenth and beginning of the eighteenth centuries in the United States. As the families prospered, the original one-room space often became the kitchen wing of a larger two-story residence. The 1939 Barnett House (pages 104–109) is emblematic of the group of houses Colcord built in this style. When

Peggy Irvine furnished the home
with Priscilla draperies and an
abundance of colorful, hand-
hooked rugs.

Colcord designed Irvine House, one-story residences were increasing popular and the home's one-story massing follows this trend.

From the mid-1930s on, Los Angeles architectural designer Cliff May was perfecting the one-story California ranch house, with the main rooms oriented to the rear garden rather than the public front yard, a concept that had its origins in the California missions. At Irvine House the U-shaped floor plan wraps around a terrace with the same concept in mind.

Most of Colcord's signature Colonial Revival features appear here: some exterior walls veneered with stone to simulate masonry construction, others sheathed with wooden clapboard or board-and-batten siding, covered porches with elliptical arches supported by slender wood posts, paneled shutters painted white, and wood-louvered shutters painted dark green, a wooden picket fence to frame the whole, and, a post with a Colonial-style lantern attached near the front porch.

Inside, Colcord merged the Colonial Revival look with contemporary trends, such as knotty pine paneling in the den. The room's large fireplace is a copy of kitchen fireplaces where meals were prepared. His design added a wrought-iron trammel and a cast-iron kettle for an authentic look. A reproduction tin lantern on the fireplace mantel carried the conceit further; it's attached permanently to the shelf and electrified to become a light fixture.

Kitchens at the beginning of the twentieth century were austere workspaces, but in the late 1920s colorful decorative tile and finishes were introduced. Colcord's plans for the kitchen followed this new approach that gave it greater importance. He introduced Colonial Revival architectural details to match the rest of the house: a mantle shelf around the stove hood, and tongue-and-groove cabinet doors with wrought-iron hardware.

The interior furnishings are characteristic of pieces from 1790 to 1840. The Hitchcock-style bench in the entry hall and the painted Windsor chairs in the dining room are representative of the "fancy" painted furniture used in place of fine mahogany furniture. The hand-hooked rugs would have been made

1940   Commissioned by the Irvine Family
Date Unknown Granted to John Fitzgerald
1986   Granted to Union Bank, Trustee of
          the John Fitzgerald Trust
1988   Granted to R. Keith Dresser
1994   Granted to Jolie A. Chain
1997   Granted to Anne J. & Waylon C. Green
2003   Granted to James S. Rosenfield

2,293 square feet; 30,488-square-foot lot
3 bedrooms; 4 bathrooms
Builder: unknown
1941 photography: Maynard L. Parker

The heart of this house is a light-filled den overlooking the backyard and a creek beyond. Above the desk is a secret panel pass-through to the kitchen.

in one's own home with patterns that imitated high-style carpets in the living spaces of the upper classes, and the wall covering in the dining room is historically correct for the second quarter of the nineteenth century when mass-produced wallpaper became available. Collecting early-nineteenth-century pressed glass, seen here in the entry window (page 31), became popular in the 1930s.

Filmmaker Jolie Chain, the house's fourth owner, felt compelled to keep Colcord's look fully intact. She learned about its significance while visiting producer Tony Thomas' Pennsylvania Dutch Colcord in Beverly Hills. "Since my father was the head of a wrecking company years ago, I thought it was good karma to care for this beautiful home," she said. Real estate developer James Rosenfield is the current steward of Irvine House. He has made several meticulous improvements, but only, he believes, those that Colcord would have approved.

The Colcord
trademark bed
alcove is adjacent
to the Victorian-
style fireplace
surround and
sitting area.

WOLF HOUSE
BEL-AIR, 1949

Three Patterns for Traditional

In the years following the Second World War, Colcord expanded his focus from designing traditional Revival-style properties to another vernacular he termed "Country Colonials." These historically imprecise and more organically interpreted versions of East Coast Colonial Revival homes became the architect's calling card. In fact, between 1945 and 1983 he designed dozens of them. Further, Colcord's new style could easily adapt to irregular, yet spacious building lots that became available on newly opened tracts in Beverly Hills, Bel-Air and the Royal Oaks section of Encino.

Many of these unconventional parcels were located on winding mountain roads, and called for floor plans with rooms radiating at angles from a main core. This seeming disadvantage proved exactly the opposite, for the abundant Southern California sunshine poured in through windows placed in the resulting wings. Sylvan Wolf, an awards and medals manufacturer, and his wife, lived in nearby Cheviot Hills; they purchased one of

Top: The *Los Angeles Times* "Home" section featured Wolf House on several covers. *Right and opposite:* The contrast between the past and present façade photographs show that little has changed in fifty-nine years.

Right: A 1949 photograph of the living room shows exactly how the house looked when Mr. & Mrs. Sylvan Wolf and their son Melford, a Helms-trophy winner, occupied it. *Opposite:* In 2007, little has changed besides the furnishings.

these hillside-hugging lots where Colcord's nostalgic design felt airy and informal.

Outside, Colcord mixed clapboards, stone, and board-and-batten siding. Marking the asymmetrical front entry are delicate segmental arches and a Colonial-style dough trough utilized as a planter box. Colcord repeated his favored pre-war motifs: a fieldstone porch sheathed in cement plaster to simulate protective lime wash, a flagstone porch floor, a paneled front door painted white, and a period-correct lantern.

Not to be forgotten was the influence of the automobile, which played a central role in the organization of Colcord's ranch houses and most other homes built after 1945. The driveway and garage, which previously were placed to the side and/or back of the property, were relocated to the front of the residence to provide direct access from the car to the house via the kitchen.

Principal living spaces inside were relocated to the back of the house and open out to a terrace and private garden. Bedrooms, once relegated to upper floors, were now on the ground level and less private. The kitchen and service wing moved to the front of the residence and were integrated into the public areas. This hierarchy of space is much more casual and reflected changes in family life, post-war, as live-in servants were no longer a part of most households.

Inside there are three fireplaces—all much larger than found in his pre-war houses—along with beamed ceilings, hand-textured plaster walls, random plank floors, and generous windows and Dutch doors to admit prized views. After Wolf

1948   Commissioned by Mr. & Mrs. Sylvan J. Wolf
1976   Granted to Elaine & Robert Ellison

3,643 square feet; 35,719-square-foot lot
3 bedrooms; 4 bathrooms
1948 acquisition cost: $9,500
Builder: The Warmington Company
1949 photography: Robert C. Cleveland
2007 photography: Mary E. Nichols

House was severely damaged by the 1961 Bel-Air fire, the Wolfs immediately rebuilt almost exactly according to the original plans, a testament to the original design concept.

In 1976, the home was purchased by producer and Emmy-winning comedy writer Robert Ellison and his wife Elaine, a former model. "Bob and I were both born and raised in New York City and never thought about living anywhere else," explains Elaine. "Besides a Manhattan apartment, our dream was to own a traditional farmhouse somewhere in upstate New York or Connecticut and spend weekends there." Work brought the Ellisons to California, but their longing for a country house lingered. Since they would be staying on the West Coast longer than anticipated, Elaine began quietly looking for a home: "I toured this house, felt an instant connection to it, and so did Bob. Unfortunately, it was out of our price range, but we admired it so much that we made an offer anyway. Luckily for us it was accepted!"

With the move finished, they called interior designer John Hall for help. "At the time, Bob wrote episodes of the *Mary Tyler Moore Show* and we learned about John from Mary, and her show's producer Allan Burns. John updated the cabana and created a wonderful new area to entertain guests. Maxine Smith designed our bedroom suite and more

Above: The combination dining room and den overlooks the Bel-Air Country Club. *Opposite:* The garden has matured and offers a beautiful backdrop against the rich, hand-hewn wood interior.

recently designer Doug Marsceill has helped us with everything else."

Bob says that he and Elaine visit lots of beautiful houses, "but when we walk through our front door, we realize how much we love our home. We appreciate the craftsmanship so much that we recently decided not to install a new plasma TV as it just wouldn't be in keeping with the feel of the rooms."

The Ellisons' dream of a home in the country came true more than decades ago. It simply turned out to be in a different neighborhood; three thousand miles west of New England in the storied hills of Bel-Air, where they have nurtured this enchanted estate ever since.

Top: The breakfast nook opens into the kitchen.
Below: Constructed of knotty pine, the open, servantless kitchen shows the new way of living post-World War II.

The bar, which remains in flawless condition, was "party central" according to frequent guest Sally Queen, whose husband William was Melford Wolf's best friend.

NAUMANN HOUSE
BEVERLY HILLS, 1949

Below: Colcord converted an Oriental screen into bi-fold doors to separate the foyer from the living room for the owner, who was an importer of Asian artifacts.
Opposite: The exterior of Naumann House is a blend of Hollywood Regency and New Orleans-style design.

In the post-World War II years, Colcord was clearly exploring new design directions. Shifting from his command of period revivalism, he designed an exceedingly high-style house for Carl Naumann, an importer of Asian artifacts, and his wife Elizabeth. Obviously, the well-traveled couple's Asian lamps and screens would probably not harmonize with one of Colcord's Country Colonials.

The impact of architect Paul Williams' 1930s-era, neo-Regency alterations and additions for the Saks Fifth Avenue store in Beverly Hills and his addition to the Beverly Hills Hotel is unmistakable here. Colcord delineates a steeply-pitched hip roof embellished with sheet-metal finials at the ridge, and a broad piazza extending across the front of the house with wrought-iron supports reminiscent of elegant wrought- and cast-iron balconies in New Orleans. The elongated sash windows reach almost to the floor of the piazza and decorative brickwork is found at the top of the exterior walls and on the chimneystack.

The dining room is beautifully proportioned with a dome ceiling.

Interior details display an entirely new aesthetic that has references to the sophistication of 1930s Moderne and the exotic character of Asian decorative arts at Naumann House. This direction separates the treatment of the interiors from the architectural style of the exterior, which was unusual for Colcord's projects up to this point.

Moldings around the living room window casings and fireplace surround have no historical references, and gold-veined mirrors over the fireplace, a fashionable new material in the late 1940s, are unexpected. They are cousin to architectural details in Paul Williams' Polo Lounge or in the Sunset Strip design salon of William Haines, the actor-turned-interior decorator who was winning prestigious commissions on the Westside of Los Angeles for entertainment world luminaries.

The fashionably popular decorator Elizabeth McPherson was engaged to design not only the interior shell, but the furniture as well. She installed indirect lighting filtered through Lucite rods, and abandoned hardwood floors, as passé as Colonial lanterns, in favor of wall-to-wall carpeting, the only desirable floor covering of the time. Asian decorative arts, like Haines used and preferred by the Naumanns, added an exotic and sophisticated note.

This home has been exquisitely maintained by the current owners, doctors Laura and Bob Audell. Architect Ward Jewell, who enlarged the home in the 1990s, says: "This is indeed a unique home for Colcord since it departs from his typical country English genre with its usual blend of stylistic references. Naumann House is based upon a classical French axial floor plan for the organization of the main public spaces. Colcord then 'coats' the rooms with clean and simple Moderne detailing and casework. Somehow all of these seemingly disparate ideas coalesce in what is actually a simple and extremely well-proportioned whole. It was definitely a surprise for me to discover that this wonderful home was designed by Colcord."

1949 Commissioned by Elizabeth & Carl Naumann
1983 Granted to Debra V. & Wilmore B. Finerman
1994 Granted to Laura G. & Robert A. Audell

3,663 square feet; 17,468-square-foot lot
3 bedrooms; 4 bathrooms
1949 permit valuation, $60,250; land cost $23,000
Builder: unknown
1949 photography: Maynard L. Parker

The coved ceiling in the living room hides a sophisticated theater-style lighting system still in operation today. Flanking the fireplace are hand-carved, sage green-colored granite pilasters.

GORDEAN HOUSE
BEVERLY HILLS, 1951

Below: Gordean House is unusual because the garage was placed at the front of the house, an adaptation that signals the importance of the automobile after World War II. Residents Tony Curtis and Janet Leigh enlarged the home in the 1960s. *Opposite:* At the time that Colcord designed Gordean House, the swimming pool was becoming an integrated part of affluent households. Two neighboring homes (background and top) were also designed by Colcord in the newly-developed Coldwater Canyon neighborhood.

At Gordean House, Colcord was still faithful to Period Revival designs, but changing lifestyles, new materials, and innovative building features compelled him to redefine his post-war Colonial-style architecture. The home for Isadore Gordean, an importer and land developer, and his wife Nettie, retains architectural features associated with Colcord's houses in the 1930s and early 1940s, but these features tend to be larger and less detailed than the eighteenth-century Colonial-style elements Colcord adapted prior to 1945. Colcord wasn't alone—the loose interpretation of period details is a defining aspect of many houses built in the 1950s.

The most noticeable difference is in the massing and configuration, which is much heavier than in Colcord's earlier Colonial Revival houses. Wide use of large, double-window dormers, introduced in the twentieth century, create a more massive appearance than the lighter, single-window dormers typical in the eighteenth century. The stone veneer

on Colcord's earlier houses had pointed edges so the mortar filled the joints between the masonry. The pointing on Gordean House was eliminated in order to articulate the individual stones. This technique is typical of stone veneers used extensively on ranch houses constructed in the 1950s.

One of Colcord's most recognizable touches, slender supports for covered porch roofs, is used only on the porch adjacent to the garage. In contrast, at the entrance, he introduced lattice panels that appear more substantial. Positioning the garage in the front of the house rather than at the back of the property was an additional significant change. Automobiles were now essential and it was easier to park them in a garage near the street as opposed to navigating down a long, narrow driveway. Locating garages in the front also released more space for lawns and swimming pools in the backyards.

Inside, a playroom replaced the cozy libraries and dens found in Colcord's pre-war residences. The playroom is significantly sized because it had become a family's primary gathering place. After two decades of limitations forced by the Great Depression and the Second World War, the notion of a playful family in itself represents a great change in the approach to life. It also became home to new built-in television cabinets, an entirely new furniture form. Colcord linked the past to the future with the Colonial-style, knotty pine entertainment center—he recognized the dominating role of television in family life.

The playroom's sliding-glass doors were another innovation of the early 1950s and were an innovative improvement over traditional wood French doors. Although the doors at Gordean House were steel, most sliding doors were made of aluminum, which was a relatively new material. This metal was developed for military use during the war and was one of many products that industry borrowed for new uses in the post-war years. This lightweight metal made it possible to create larger openings, required minimal maintenance and was relatively inexpensive.

1950   Commissioned by Isadore C. Gordean
1952   Granted to Julia B. & Frank Sale
1961   Granted to Nettie L. & Isadore C. Gordean
1963   Granted to Tony Curtis
1965   Granted to Laura & Francis F. Quittner
1972   Granted to Stanley E. Brown
1989   Granted to Patricia B. & Marc Myers
2002   Granted to Romy E. & David Cohen

5,227 square feet; 14,039-square-foot lot
3 bedrooms; 7 bathrooms
1951 permit valuation, $49,500 + $4,950 for pool;
land cost $22,500
Builder: unknown
1951 photography: Robert C. Cleveland

The playroom, adjacent to the living room and kitchen, incorporated a large fireplace punctuated with the "Colcord Beam."

Another view of the playroom shows the use of modern materials. A steel-framed sliding-glass door allows unobstructed Pacific Ocean views. Ironically, a subsequent owner replaced the sliding door with traditional paned windows and French doors.

Colcord also reacted to the popularity of the barbeque phenomenon, another change in American life. Before the war, cooking outdoors happened on a grill out-of-doors. For most homeowners in the 1950s cooking on an outdoor grill was an entirely new idea, and the fact that this activity was considered to be a man's role was even more surprising. However, Colcord's built-in grill *inside* the house was extraordinary and would still be reserved for privileged families for several more decades.

Current residents Romy and David Cohen, who moved from Connecticut, desired a home that communicated casual and gracious living, which to them was an unpretentious family house with a New England sensibility. David, president of a residential construction firm, said: "We had a few specific requirements such as a home that was well built, thoughtfully designed, had good natural light and took into account the site and surroundings. We happily found it. Further, regarding the surroundings, we are reminded of living in Hollywood each month as magazines addressed to Tony Curtis—who owned the home in the 1960s—still arrive. We love living here and entertaining family and friends—they know they are coming to a home and not just a house."

The playroom featured a rarity for the time: a home-entertainment system. The custom-built cabinet, most likely manufactured by Avery Rennick in West Hollywood, housed a turntable, radio, television and speakers.

HAWKINS HOUSE
Beverly Hills, 1953

I n the early 1950s, Colcord's clients continued to request traditional homes, but contemporary architecture, modern taste, and new building materials were beginning to change the historic appearance of his houses.

Eugene A. Hawkins, Jr., a prominent attorney, and his wife Margaret lived nearby in Beverly Hills when they purchased a stunning view property in a new development carved from the estate of the late Silsby M. Spalding, a former mayor of Beverly Hills. Hawkins House whispers Colcord's unmistakable hand throughout, though he added many contemporary motifs rarely associated with his work until this time. The façade of Hawkins House has Colcord's familiar double-hung sash windows and a paneled door with a glazed transom. But not-so-subtle differences make this house appear significantly unlike his Colonial Revivals from the 1930s and early 1940s.

The large pyramidal roof and center chimney over the entrance are particularly bold changes. Colcord took the traditional hip roof and abstracted its essence, resulting in this strong geometrical form. The massing of the roofs and the strong delineation of the thick, heavy shingles recalls roofs not from the Pennsylvania countryside but from the English colony of Bermuda. For another perspective, the *Los Angeles Times*, prior to construction, described the house as "French New Orleans."

The covered walkway between the kitchen and the garage is the most startling juxtaposition between modern and traditional. The sinuous line of the structure and the clean lines of its flat roof would look suitable outside any high-style, mid-century modern building in Los Angeles and reflects

Through the steel-framed dining room window there is a clear view of the serpentine-shaped colonnade linking the home to the garage and guesthouse.

Perched on a true "King of the Hill" parcel, Hawkins House offers impressive vistas of the Los Angeles basin. The colonnade, with trellised supports, parallels the motor court and frames the stunning views.

the undeniable influence of International Style on Southern California architects after the Second World War.

While the walkway may appear incongruous, close inspection reveals that the contemporary roof is supported by decorative wrought-iron panels similar to those the architect used to support the piazza roof on the 1949 Naumann House (pages 130–133).

Inside, the floor plan is also a departure. The traditional formal hierarchy of clearly defined spaces found in Colcord's previous work has been replaced by spacious rooms featuring large picture windows. They express the informality of the modern movement, and, take advantage of privileged, dazzling views. Steel sliding doors, which first appeared two years earlier at Gordean House (pages 134–139), are now used as windows in the dining room. The combination of traditional moldings and sliding windows demonstrate how contemporary materials and architectural details were added to traditional houses without any sense of irony.

Current residents Carrie and Bernie Brillstein were married at Hawkins House just as the twentieth century ended. Bernie Brillstein, one of Hollywood's most illustrious talent managers, is no stranger to fine homes. When he first moved to Beverly Hills in the late 1960s, he purchased a Colcord Farmhouse-style home and then later moved to a multi-acre, Paul Williams Georgian-style estate, owned at different times by the Bill Cosby and Michael Landon families.

The Brillsteins' favorite part of Hawkins House is the warmth and comfort it always brings. Carrie Brillstein observes that "It never feels too large for the two of us, yet it accommodates the whole family whenever needed. We actually use every room and keep finding new spots to get cozy in. We often say to each other that we don't want a second home since we never want to leave this one for very long."

1953	Commissioned by Margaret J. & Eugene A. Hawkins, Jr.
1979	Granted to Hallwood Estates Limited
1983	Granted to Wicker, Inc., a Liberian Corporation
1985	Granted to George & Linda Segal
1988	Granted to Diane J. & Charles Ross Dawson
1997	Granted to Carrie & Bernard Brillstein

4,218 square feet; 35,196-square-foot lot
5 bedrooms; 6 bathrooms
Builder: Walter J. Drazan
2007 photography: Mary E. Nichols

WING HOUSE
Palos Verdes Estates, 1968

Below: Situated on the rugged coastline of the Pacific Ocean, Wing House truly commands its stirring site. This nearly seven-thousand-square-foot estate is still prized by the Palos Verdes Estates community.

Opposite: Colcord created more renderings for this home than any other of the four hundred homes he designed during his career.

When he was nearly sixty-eight years old, Colcord designed a spectacular oceanfront manor for Betty and George Wing in Palos Verdes Estates. When completed, Wing House quickly gained landmark status throughout the community and four decades later is still one of the most admired homes ever built on the peninsula.

A year after they were married, the Wings booked a vacation trip to Paris. A quick tour through the French countryside was scheduled; however, this architectural field trip turned into months and it wasn't long before the couple realized they desired a French-style home of their own.

As a child, Betty would visit her great uncle whose home sat amid an orange grove at the end of a lane behind the Beverly Hills Hotel. When it was time to find an architect to bring the couple's vision of an eighteenth-century French house to life, she remembered a nearby Colcord home which she had admired. That memory, along with designer friends' recommendations, led the couple to the still-active architect.

Although Colcord wasn't known for a formal French idiom, the couple knew that he was the perfect architect for them. "Gerry met me at the building site and we clicked right away," said Betty. "He showed me plans for Debbie Reynolds' home and another set of plans for Kirk Douglas' pool house. He quoted Mr. Douglas as saying, 'Make it biggggggggg.' Gerry always reminded me of Douglas Fairbanks, Jr., as he was very dapper, self-effacing and modest." After the plans were reviewed, the Palos Verdes Art Council wrote the Wings a letter stating that Colcord's architectural renderings were the finest ones anyone had ever submitted. Every single detail of the house had a working drawing, which was highly unusual.

Because the enclave's architectural style is predominantly Mediterranean, Wing House is something of an anomaly. An immediate neighbor told the couple he put a 'whammy' on their house. Betty Wing recalls his saying, "If you're going to build a house like that, why don't you go to Bel-Air and do it? That's no kind of house for Palos Verdes." I replied, "Unless my knowledge of geography is wrong, the Mediterranean Sea flows by the country of France, too."

Colcord used a relatively straightforward architectural vocabulary for Wing House. The steeply pitched gable roofs decorated with small finials, casement windows with small panes and the introduction of elliptical heads on the first-floor windows, and second-floor dormer windows with metal roofs, are typically French. The French Rococo entrance, with a neo-Classical aedicule (architectural frame) around the doorway, paneling on the double entrance doors, and the sinuous lines of the window on the second floor emulate pure French design.

The main block is symmetrical along an axis that extends through the entry and

1967   Land granted to Betty R. & George S. Wing
1985   Granted to Eva Gae & William J. Winn
1993   Granted to Umran Uzumcu
2005   Granted to Melahat Uzumcu & Nihat Kocarslan
2007   Granted to Melahat Uzumcu

6,862 square feet; 32,609-square-foot lot
6 bedrooms; 7 bathrooms
Builder: George Shoemaker

PLAN OF LIBRARY

SCALE 1/4" = 1'-0"

40" MAPS 40"

BOOKS BOOKS BOOKS

BOOKS

DOWN

SLIDING DOORS

HALL

T.V. CAB. UNDER GLOBE

BALCONY

MUSIC CAB.

BOOKS

REFRIG. STORAGE UNDER CAST STONE

BAR SINK

SHELVES

LIVING RM.

GRC

living room, but the plan and massing of the side wings are informal and reflect the more casual approach found in many of Colcord's rambling one-story houses. The elliptical plan foyer and the elliptic niche in the dining room echo geometric forms in neo-Classical architecture.

Inside, the romantic lines of the cantilevered staircase and Rococo wrought-iron railing are based on mid-eighteenth-century grand staircases in the great hotels built for aristocrats in Paris. The flavor of the period is emphasized by a wood-parquet floor and the wrought-iron-and-glass lantern suspended from the second-floor ceiling. The Rococo theme is carried into the living room by the marble fireplace, over-mantle, coved ceiling and French doors.

"We did not intend to build a spectacle," said Betty. "We wanted a house with space for our kids when they came home from school, and we wanted a guest room. We were not in a mood to impress anyone. We wanted it simply for our own pleasure."

The Wings named their home even before construction began. Their driver in France insisted that any principal house must have a name. On June 10, 1967 he christened their home-to-be *Les Ailes de la Mer*—The Wings of the Sea—referring to both the white caps on the Pacific Ocean and, of course, to the couple's last name.

Top: The rococo-styled balustrade gracefully curves upward, leading to three bedroom suites.
Bottom: The living room terrace looks out on the Pacific Ocean.
Opposite: The floor plan for the first and second floors follows a classic axial design. Not shown is the lower level with a billiards room clad in logs to resemble a rustic cabin.

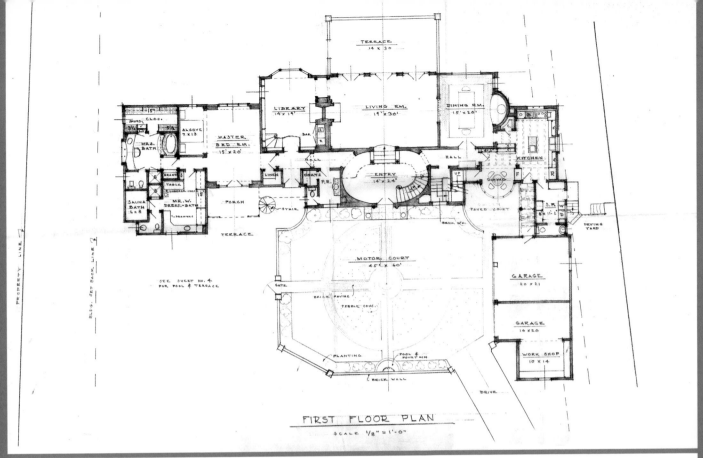

FIRST FLOOR PLAN

Scale 1/8" = 1'-0"

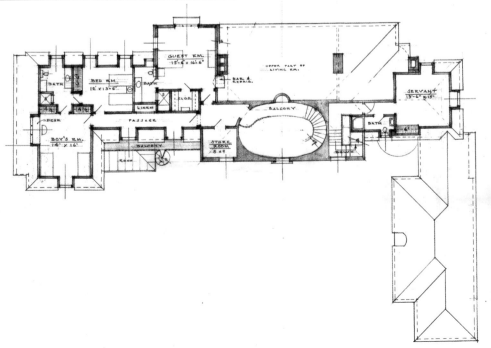

SECOND FLOOR PLAN

STERN HOUSE
STUDIO CITY, 1972

Above and cover:
Stern House is very secluded in a verdant canyon minutes from Studio City.
Opposite: **The massive living room resembles a gentleman's hunting lodge and incorporates numerous seating and entertaining areas.**

At age seventy, Colcord designed Stern House, an adaptation of a rural English cottage brimming with charming details—from the used-brick façade to numerous fireplaces and cozy window seats inside. With details from seventeenth, eighteenth, and nineteenth-century English-style architecture, this home commands its promontory setting in a sycamore-studded canyon. The house is marked by many of Colcord's design trademarks from his projects fifty years earlier as well as trends that began in the early 1960s.

In 1968, twenty-six-year-old Stephanie Sax contemplated the kind of house she wanted to build and subsequently searched out and photographed homes in Los Angeles that appealed to her. Two years later, while a guest at Connie Wald's home in Beverly Hills (pages 104–109), she learned about Colcord, who had designed the Wald residence thirty years earlier. Completely enchanted, Stephanie commissioned him to build her family's dream house in 1971. During the first meeting, she learned that almost all of the pictures she had taken were of homes designed years earlier by Colcord.

"During the early stages of designing our home," Stephanie said, "my ex-husband and I visited Mr. Colcord's surprisingly small office where I gave him my photographs and a copy of *Architectural Digest* featuring Ingrid Bergman's European home—a personal favorite. I was taken with Mr. Colcord's personal charm, as well as his beautiful drawings. I mentioned the things I liked and he immediately sketched them. Months later, when the house was being framed, we considered adding an additional garage space. He produced a finished drawing in about ten seconds on the back of an old blueprint so I could see what the finished result would look like."

The interior aspects of Stern House reflect Colcord's use of period details that reinforce the architecture of the house. The exposed post-and-beam system in the living room uses materials with the appropriate hand-hewn texture. Almost all of the beams in the living room offer structural support; only two are decorative. The bar that had been "tucked

BROOKDALE ROAD ELEVATION

ASHDALE LANE ELEVATION

GARDEN ELEVATION

Colcord's rendered façades are identical to the constructed home.

away" prior to the Second World War is now a prominent feature sharing priority with a walk-in fireplace. By the 1970s, sitting at the bar had replaced being served from the bar.

The home embraces the informality associated with mid-twentieth-century houses. The utilitarian kitchen of the 1930s and 1940s emerged as a primary area of the house with its own decorative motifs, not simply a space relegated to servants. Here, a center island with prep sink and a place to sit encourages family members and guests to pull up a seat and visit. A large grill in the kitchen fireplace is modeled after the open fireplace associated with the late seventeenth to eighteenth centuries, which held a spit for roasting, a trammel for holding a kettle, and a built-in brick oven. The use of a single post supporting the corner of the fireplace is a post-modern detail borrowed from the avant-garde style fashionable in the 1970s.

Stephanie says that she "often finds notes in the mailbox asking about the house—requests to see

1972 Commissioned by Stephanie & Joel Sax
1993 Granted to Stephanie & Jerry Stern

4,697 square feet; 19,637-square-foot lot
4 bedrooms; 5 bathrooms
Builder: Leon Slavin
2007 photography: Mary E. Nichols

Colcord designed the kitchen fireplace
to incorporate a grill. The charming
sitting area overlooks the terrace and
the pool beyond, both reached via a
wide Dutch door.

153

The dining room accommodates
a casual buffet as shown here, or
comfortably seats sixteen for a
Thanksgiving feast. Dappled garden
light streams through the leaded-glass
bay window.

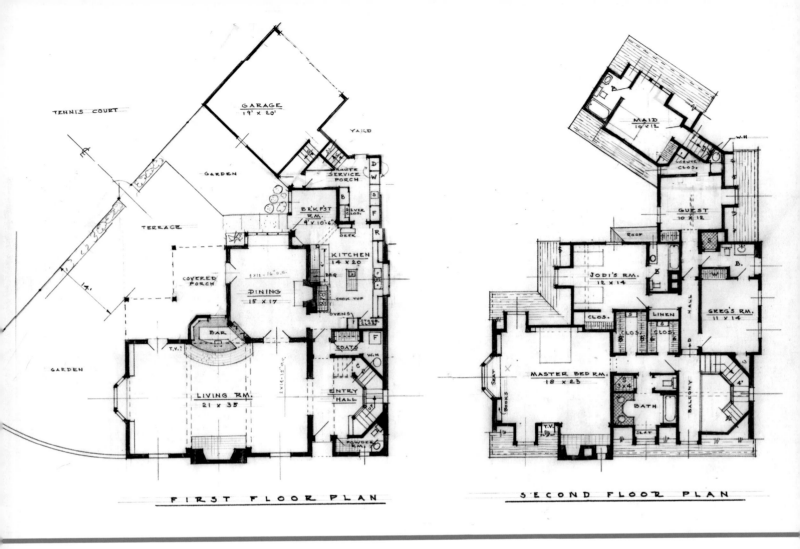

FIRST FLOOR PLAN

SECOND FLOOR PLAN

The exterior belies the actual size of Stern House, clearly shown in these plans.

the interior or to ask if we would ever consider selling. Many commercials were shot here over the years, but we had to stop that practice when a film crew decided to have their 'wrap party' in the kitchen. Too many drinks! While the crew removed their gaffer's tape they simultaneously ripped off strips of wallpaper. The margarita blenders never stopped!"

After raising two children, Stephanie and her husband divorced; she retained the house. "I reconnected with a terrific man from my college days, Jerry Stern. In early 1992 we threw a Valentine's Day party for our families and friends. Near the end of the evening, Jerry walked me over to the piano, next to the famous "Colcord Beam" fireplace, and in front of eighty guests asked me to marry him. I was happily shocked, said yes, and we married a year later. For that reason, and many more, this home will always be magical to me."

STERN HOUSE

AFTERWORD

When I heard Bret Parsons talk about how much he loves the work of architect Gerard R. Colcord, I knew there would be at least a partial answer, sooner rather than later, to one of the more vexing questions I regularly ask myself as a real estate reporter, which is:

"Where in the world is there more information on the architects and others who have designed some of the finest homes in California?"

In my job at the *Los Angeles Times*, almost every week I faced the problem of not having enough information on these fellows (indeed, there weren't many women architects in the formative years of California architecture) to write a "Hot Property" or "Home of the Week" column. I have been amazed to find how little is known about even some of the bigger names in architecture such as Colcord.

Thank goodness for Bret. And I welcome him to what I call "keepers of the flame."

There aren't enough of them. In my nearly thirty years of writing about real estate at the *Times*, I've personally known only two—Wally Neff, son of architect Wallace Neff, and Karen Hudson, granddaughter of architect Paul R. Williams. For keepers of the flame, it's a labor of love to create a book about someone whose work is as admired as Colcord's. Bret is passionate about research and this book. And so it was no surprise to me that his appreciation of fine houses tracks back to his own drawings in kindergarten. Colcord, too, was an artist.

No doubt keepers of the flame help keep the work of notable architects and others alive, but the situation is still "not good enough." You can research all day and night, but if there isn't anything in the files and nothing on the bookshelves, you're out of luck.

Memory eventually dies and with it goes anecdotes about who designed what and why. John Lautner's work is already getting shorter shrift than it should. And Cliff May, not an architect, but a design figure worth remembering, could be forgotten as father of the California ranch-style house. Thank goodness there's a book on his work. Does it

Colcord designed Lilly House, located in Mandeville Canyon, in 1964. In forty years it has had only two owners.

matter? Perhaps not in some places, but it should in Southern California. Where else is there such a rich assortment of architectural styles and stories, often connected with Hollywood? Where else are so many people interested in real estate?

I think of that on weekends when I join thousands of "Looky Lous" touring open houses. Then I wonder: where else does the weather help to perpetuate such a pleasant and informative way to spend an afternoon? Maybe Bret will inspire some of these inspectors to spend the next morning recording what they learned. If we who love notable homes are lucky, he will inspire himself to make his book on Colcord the first of many about architects who designed the houses we can still see.

RUTH RYON
Redondo Beach

ʃ

ACKNOWLEDGMENTS

Team Colcord:

Angel City Press: Paddy Calistro, Scott McAuley, Jim Schneeweis, Chuck Morrell, Theresa Accomazzo

Amy Inouye of Future Studio, book design

Robin Evens, Web site design

John David Hough, images

Art Gontier, weathervane rendering

Jackie Green, public relations

Betty Goodwin, editing

Mary E. Nichols, photography

Drew Poley, PowerPoint presentations

Stephan Sie, computer programming

Martin Eli Weil, AIA, architectural research

Old Republic Title Company: Linda Michele, Guido Schenkhuizen, Rand Traverse

Thank you to past and present Colcord residents:

Maud Adams
Courtney Newhart Albertini
Raphie Aronowitz
Laura & Robert Audell
Gail & Robert Bardin
Margaret Beckendorf
Judith & Ralph Benner
John C. Bercsi
Adrea & Sandy Bettelman
Lynne & Herb Binder
Carolyn Blackburn & Ira Land
Nancy Sue Blumenfeld
Gladys Boynton
Carrie & Bernie Brillstein
Marilyn Buck
Hollenbeck & Rodney Buck
Elizabeth Bury
Ryan Cassidy
Jolie Chain
Whitney Chase & Tom Chasin
Romy & David Cohen
Toni & Bruce Corwin
Karen Bell & Rob Cox
Wim de Wit
Peter W. Douglas, Jr.
Alison & Michael Druyanoff
Elaine & Bob Ellison
Wendy Finerman
PJ & Randall Fink
Alan Finkel
Bob Finkel
Harrison Ford
Barbara & Simon Gamer
Marilyn Garber
Jo Ann & Terry Gloege
Shirl Goedike
Suzanne Goldstein
Kathy Gormly
Tricia & Jeff Graup
Marjorie Greenberg
Jo Haldeman
Marjorie Hansen
Goldyne Zimet Hearsh
Barbara Hillman
Marcia Hobbs
Jan & Rick Holz
Bill Horton, Jr.
Carol & Art Hurt
Alana & Michael Jackson
Shirley Jones
Glorya Kaufman
Deb Lacusta
David Ladd
Margaret & Tom Larkin
Mary Ann & George Leal
William (Bill) Lusk
Mary & Dana Martin
Nancy & Zubin Mehta
Patty & Mark Meyers
Kathy & Chase Morgan

Larry Murphy
Ginnie & Bob Newhart
Nevin & Ted Pallad
Ann & Ronald Whitford Paul
Donald R. Pennell
Amy & Bob Perille
Leonora & Arthur Rasmussen
Mary Robin Redd
Leland J. Reicher
Mariana & Arthur Reilly
James S. Rosenfield
Diane & Sol Rosenthal
Peggy & Harvey Saferstein
Ben Sandler
Evelyn & Edward Schwartz
Lori Shearing
Ralph M. Singer
Stephanie & Jerry Stern
Rita & Scott Sternberg
Kris Sommer &
    Richard Stevenson
Susan Sullivan
Debbie & Eric Swanson
Andrew Wald
Connie Wald
Robert Wald
Jobeth Williams & John Pasquin
Betty Wing
Linda & Larry Wolf
Toni Wright
Bonnie & Paul Yaeger
Gloria Yaeger
Marcia Ziffren

**In appreciation to
Colcord friends:**

Rita Amendola
Christine Anderson
Marc Appleton
Ann Ascher
Joe Babajian & Darren Cardona
Mila & Richard Bonner
Tim Barber
Tom Buckley
John Cottrell
John Crosse
Brett Dillenberg
Krista & John Everage
Peri Gilpin
Jody Greenwald
Carl Jespersen
Larry Laughlin
Thomas Lavin
Nelda Linsk
Marion Lowry
Mort Lowy
Doug Marsceill
Betty Ann Marshall
Elizabeth McMillian
Marian Miller
Karyn R. Millet
Laura Montalban
Pat Montandon
Michael Murray
Joe Nye
Shirley Parsons
Tal Parsons
Sally Queen

Gregg Rennick
Virginia Rennick
Phyllis Cole Rowen
Barbara & Joe Ruggiero
Elaine, Warren & Kenny Selko
Dawn Shobe & Family
Ed Solorzano
Tim Steele
Ron Stevens
M. Brian Tichenor
Catherine Vandecasteele
Mitch Waldstein
Kathryn Waltzer
Jim Warmington
Gerald (Jerry) Washington
Tom Watson
Henry Weaks

Beverly Hills Public Library
Culver Military Academy
Friends of Gamble House
Huntington Library
Institute of Classical Architecture
    & Classical America
Los Angeles Conservancy
Pacific Design Center
San Marino Historical Society
USC School of Architecture

IMAGE CREDITS

Robert C. Cleveland: 39–43

Culver Military Academy: 19

Karyn Millet: 6–7

Los Angeles Times: 122

Pat Montandon: 12

Mott Studios: 4, 17, 23

Mary E. Nichols: cover, 11, 13, author's photo

Maynard L. Parker: 8, 9, 26, 27, 29, 31

Bret Parsons: 14, 35 (top)

Jeanne Peet-Thompson/ Paula Tebbe: 157

Joel Phillips: 37

Marianna Reilly: 35 (bottom)

Stephanie Stern: 16, 22, 152

Betty Wing: 144, 148

W. P. Woodcock: back cover, 15, 25

All other images, renderings and photos contained in this book were supplied by Liza Kent.

Colcord Home
Copyright © 2008 by Bret Parsons

Designed by Amy Inouye, www.futurestudio.com

10 9 8 7 6 5 4 3 2 1

ISBN-13 978-1-883318-88-8 / ISBN-10 1-883318-88-2

Library of Congress Cataloging-in-Publication Data

Parsons, Bret.
 Colcord : home / by Bret Parsons.
   p. cm.
 Summary: "1920s Southern California was the greatest home-building region in the world. Beaux-Arts trained architect Gerard Colcord flourished there, creating 400 estates between 1924 and 1984. Bret Parsons culled through 10,000 original documents and interviewed 300 past and present Colcord homeowners to complete this intimate portrait of the man and his homes. Complete with architectural renderings and photographs" —Provided by publisher.
 ISBN 978-1-883318-88-8 (hardcover : alk. paper)
 1. Colcord, Gerard Rae, 1900-1984. 2. Architecture, Domestic—California, Southern. 3. Architecture—California, Southern—20th century. I. Colcord, Gerard Rae, 1900-1984. II. Title.

NA737.C637P37 2008
728.092—dc22
[B]

                    2008023643

Printed in the United States of America

ANGEL CITY PRESS
2118 Wilshire Blvd. #880
Santa Monica, California 90403
310.395.9982
www.angelcitypress.com